DR. MIRAL S MEHTA

# CHASING SUCCESS IN *High Heels*

12 FUNDAMENTAL RULES

**POWER, INFLUENCE, & SUCCESS FOR WOMEN**

Clever Fox® PUBLISHING

Chennai • Bangalore

CLEVER FOX PUBLISHING
Chennai, India

Published by CLEVER FOX PUBLISHING 2025

Hardback: 978-93-6707-347-6
Paperback: 978-93-6707-348-3

*For my parents and my grandparents*

*For raising a strong woman*

*For my husband*

*For standing by a strong woman*

*For my children*

*For being my strength*

# CONTENTS

# PREFACE

If only life would unfold the way we would like it to, then there would be no chaos, no agony. There would also be no competition, no striving, no joy of overcoming the obstacles, no sense of achievement. Being human is having the ability to dream, to desire, and being alive is having the courage to strive for those dreams.

I am one human being who is alive and constantly setting new milestones to pursue, one after the other. It was this pursuit that made me leave the contentment of a well-established career. An ophthalmologist and oculoplastic surgeon in the bustling city of Mumbai, moved to a completely new country, far away from the warmth of family, risking years of education, and safety of a lucrative established profession. My partner, a successful criminal defence lawyer in the High Court of Mumbai, showed unwavering support and confidence in *us*. Starting afresh was not something I feared – *losing* is what I feared the most. It takes a lot of courage, patience, and humility to be able to leave everything, come to a new country, and start over. Maybe it was a yearning to do more, have a bigger impact, maybe it was this crazy desire to break out of the comfort zone. It did not take a moment's hesitation to leave for new adventures, new horizons, with a new life of 32 weeks taking form inside of me. I am not sure how much we were willing to take on with this leap of faith, but I can say, it took a lot. Faith, love, courage of the unborn soul, and blessings of our ancestors- all of this fuelled our journey over the coming years.

The next few years brought an immense number of challenges, tears, and pain. With time, I realized that each one of the challenges I faced were meant to make me stronger. They were there to teach me new lessons that I needed to learn in order to get to the next phase of my growth. Never one to give up, I have always been the person that pushes through challenges or pivots. I shed some tears or let out a scream in pain and frustration, and then I move on to what needs to be done – I never give myself any other choice. Having an extremely loving, supportive father, a similarly amazing husband, and extremely mature and understanding children, has helped me gather myself every single time I felt like I was broken.

The battles I have fought have ranged from being a female professional in the industry dominated by the old boys' club to being discriminated for being an immigrant woman of colour demanding her rightful place in a high paying career – sometimes by colleagues, at other times by the Canadian regulatory bodies and professional associations. Along the way, I picked up arms against the tech giants to use data for positive outcomes for users, instead of using it to personalize marketing and advertising, and to train AI ethically. My dreams and aspirations took me across the globe to try and build a consortium for the ethical use of emerging tech, and its impact on teens and youth.

At some point in my career, I was shielding myself from the offensives from other women in the industry on the one hand, and building a decentralized health platform to empower individuals about their own healthcare on the other. I heal patients during the day, build businesses in the evening, and write at night. In between, I mentor women and youth. From a self-taught IT enthusiast in AI, blockchain, and other exponential technologies, to advocacy in education and mental health for youth, I have found myself swimming against the tide quite often.

From the depths of self doubt and isolation, to the fear of losing my identity as a physician, I tapped into every ounce of courage and faith to survive what I knew will pass. And the reward for the resilience has been more trouble. From quiet struggle to legal battles, from nursing some wounds quietly and praying in the silence of the night, to finding my voice, the strategies that came to my aid have been very diverse.

From tears and complaints and uncertain steps, to facing challenges with a belief in myself, no matter the outcome, I have come a long way. Each challenge has taught me invaluable lessons.

Sometimes the victory was sweet, other times futile. Sometimes the failures felt bitter, other times pivotal. Every single rule in this book has come to my rescue at some point in time. One of those things that you can only notice in retrospect, not while you're living it. The challenges I have faced demanded that I learn, grow, and accept. This book is a culmination of those learnings that made me tougher than my challenges.

Every goal and ambition sits in the midst of seemingly insurmountable challenges. Sometimes our fears – and sometimes circumstances – prevent us from taking the leap of faith. In the world of comfort, instant gratification, and short-term distractions, it takes patience, focus, and a sense of purpose to not abandon our path. While it was very tempting to give up and find the comfort zone of a small non-competitive corner to myself, I would ask myself what would I regret – failure, or giving up?

The choice was easy, and every time I made my decision, the Universe bestowed me with the strength and the courage to follow my dreams, and mentors to guide me along my way.

I am eternally grateful for the life with which I have been endowed – whether I am running a hyper efficient health care centre, leading or investing in multiple companies, or travelling the world with my family.

Every rule in this book was written from profound soul searching, reliving every challenge I faced, trying to extract the lessons I learnt from them, and compiling them into adaptable strategies for women to advance themselves in their fields.

Whether you are a woman in the corporate world, or someone building or scaling your own business, whether you are a woman in a male-dominated industry or are choosing to walk on the path towards one, these rules are like a compass that will help you navigate your path. In between the lessons in each of these rules, lies every type of challenge that I have faced or that you may face. Identify the ideas that seek you and leave the rest in the arsenal for future.

At the end of each chapter, I have consolidated some steps that steer you towards how to implement the lesson and translate it into real-world actions. Consider these as a shortcut to the solution that your heart is seeking and one that you can come back to.

As a society, we have long taught our children the skills to navigate a career pathway. With this book, I am hoping to expose them to the wisdom needed to overcome challenges and to navigate life. My children have been my first audience for this book, and for those on the path of conscious parenting, it is likely that you might want to read this book to your children as well. The core characteristics of a successful businessperson – and a good human being who is able to tap into their inner potential – is something that we hope to imbibe in our children. Chapters like "Believe in Yourself," "Stay True to Yourself," and "Trust Your Instincts" are key to unlocking hidden potential early on.

In a time where perfection is given a negative connotation due to the mental toll it takes, high performers and high achievers are fighting a unique inner battle. I spent half my life pursuing perfection, and the other half fighting the *urge* for perfection. As I accept myself, I realise that while I cannot leave the pursuit of perfection, I can channel it in the right way. And therefore, the birth of the "Theory of Aligned Perfection." which helps me navigate perfection more productively.

I have accomplished some goals and I have many more to fulfill. It is but a journey of a lifetime, taken in small steps. The only difference now is that I know what not to do, and I know what to prioritize. I will fumble, I will fall, but I will never give up. And in between these pages, I will take you on a journey to find the strength to do so as well.

# ACKNOWLEDGEMENTS

I am grateful for my mentors Chuck Allard and David Cote for standing by me in tough times, and believing in me, when I was having doubts. I am blessed to have a father like Savji Patel, who pampered me and nurtured me and pushed me towards my goals; and for laying the foundations of business, finance, investments and negotiations; and my late grandfather, Dungarshibhai Patel, for the challenges he took on for the family, and for his selfless love, care and generosity for everyone around him. Without both of them, I would have crumpled under pressure or would have been tempted to give up at some point in my life.

Other influential contributors to my growth are my husband Shounak Mehta, and my children Myra and Vian. They have seen me through all my ups and downs, through my tears and smiles, and have stood with me patiently while I sought out my inner strength. They know that it is not an end, just the beginning of a new journey, and new challenges.

Last but not the least, I draw courage and inspiration from my friends, who have time and again, put aside their own troubles, to be with me in mine. My close confidantes, my cheerleaders – some amazing, accomplished women, some grounded fulfilled souls, and some very close friends who have been mothers to my children while I fulfill my dreams, or have lent me an ear while I vent my frustrations. Some have quietly, with their presence, been examples of courage and character in my life. This also includes my mom, Usha Patel, for being ahead of her time and having a unique way of embracing her challenges and winning solely with love and positive intention.

RULE 1

# DEFINE YOUR DREAMS AND GO AFTER THEM

It is but an irony that the creator of man needs protection from man.

Humanity evolved and bred civilization, and now they sustain each other. Man and woman evolved into roles that were decided by the norms of the society at the time, and gradually these roles were dictated more by the circumstances that arose out of humanity's needs to expand, conquer, and control – more specifically, men's needs to do so. From survival to adventure, it was long and difficult, and the road soon became the one that cannot be traced backwards. We are creatures of habit, and habits got ingrained into lifestyles.

While adaptation came as a natural instinct for both men and women, the core nature and true desires for each were distinct. Women desire stability, safety, security, balance and compassion. They strive to nurture the community and the family, and aim for cohesion, compatibility, and egalitarianism. Men, on the other hand, gravitate towards stability with adventure, safety, and security with competition, and in doing so, balance and compassion have been replaced with survival of the fittest, and nurturing got limited to one's own.

These perspectives are two sides of the same coin, the yin and yang of the society, each incomplete without the other. These viewpoints were essential for the evolution of society, for the evolution of civilization. But while both are necessary and complimentary, the yin and the yang need to be in balance. The key is not to get more of one or the other – the key is to get each one in the right amount. And yet, over time, the need to supersede others and the need to conquer, overshadowed the need for stable growth. Throughout history, men, and their power to win and to destroy, have undermined women's calming, cohesive, quiet strength. And since then, the evolution of society has been closely entwined with the evolution of the men's needs.

* * *

Every time a woman dreams, there are millions of people around her that will tell her that she won't make it. It's as if they were all born to protect her from failure, or protect her from the struggles towards success. *A woman needs to be protected*, they think. It's not necessarily the people who mean you harm who feel this way; it could also be the very people who love you the most.

From the ancient times, women were given the responsibility of taking care of the household, feeding the children, and being a homemaker, while the men went out hunting and gathering and assuming the role of being a provider and a protector. Or that's what we are told. As we all know, history is written by the winners, as much as history is written by the rulers – rule creators and rule refiners. This history is then turned into movies, taught in schools, and partial facts then inescapably turn into complete facts solely because of the act of repetitive narration. Folklore and mythologies are assumed or portrayed as entertaining stories these days, but may as well be the truth passed down for generations without distortion by historians. Whether the distortion of facts happens because of malice or purely self-gratification, the implications it has on societies run deep.

In eastern cultures, women were just as often the torchbearers and fighters as men. Women were respected for their knowledge, and for their fearless contributions to the community. But invasions led to destruction of civilizations, and women started staying indoors, so as not to be kidnapped or used for the menial pleasures of unruly men. They also assumed the responsibility of bearing children, nurturing them, and maintaining the bloodline, amongst other things. Men hunted while women's relevance became stunted.

In the western world, the patriarchy had a different origin. Women were considered intellectually, morally, and biologically weaker than men. In many cultures – eastern as well as western – religious texts were interpreted to support the idea of male dominance. The designated roles of providers for men and caregivers for women were indoctrinated into the medieval societies, and kept women out of the rooms that discussed individual rights and reason. The philosophical, legal, and constitutional systems were built by these very men, who were raised by the patriarchal system. This system fed the men's egos, and in return they cultivated an environment where this system thrives. The intention though, I believe, was not as much to keep the women out of power, as much it was to keep men in power.

Since then, it has been a man's world in the office and out. Over the last few years, the population of men and women have become almost equal, and yet the world still sees far fewer women in the role of CEOs, CTOs, investors, physicians, accountants, and political leaders. It is one thing for someone to not *want* to take up a certain role, or aspire to do certain jobs, but its a completely different thing to not receive the opportunity to do so.

Decades of suppression, based on safety and security concerns, led to the unbefitting cautiousness that spills over into our lives today, where our loved ones try to prevent us from dreaming too big or trying to achieve seemingly Herculean goals, lest we fail and hurt ourselves in the process. Or succeed, hurt other people's egos, and then get hurt by them as well, because of their insecurities and reactions.

* * *

There is something inside a woman's heart that triggers the dreams and ambitions to flourish, despite a minimally conducive environment, and that something is called *courage*. No fallacies of the past can be bigger than the heart that carries courage – on the basis of this courage, the journey begins for a woman to bring her dream to reality.

But women who are able to get past the initial nudge put themselves at the risk of being trampled by the rules of the man's world. That thought is enough for many women to either think smaller, or let go of their dreams entirely.

Once we manage to get past the fears and the concerns of our family members, we come face-to-face with the territorial nature of man. Even though the world is big enough to accommodate everyone, our goals, our ambitions, and our dreams make people around us insecure. The most important thing that they forget is that we are trying to create our own space – *not* usurp theirs.

Abundance is the nature of the universe, and scarcity that of the human mind. This fear of scarcity, a fear of losing what is "theirs," is often a strong force behind people's actions. It unsettles them that a woman is here, having reached this point of her own accord, and is aspiring to grow. And what is the best way to stop her from growing bigger than them? They try to crush her, by maligning her reputation or getting her tangled in unnecessary complications, so she spends the rest of her career trying to unravel those tangles. Sometimes this could be an onslaught of professional or disciplinary actions, at other times a social media maligning campaign but more often than not, it is hounding her with passive aggression.

At these moments, instead of accepting less than our full dreams, it is crucial to remind ourselves of *why* those dreams are so important to us, and why our goals matter to us. Nothing of value comes easy, and that includes your dreams. Settling for less may seem attractive in times of struggle, but the joy of fulfillment is paled by the dissatisfaction of not trusting our abilities enough. The pain of incomplete actions – and the pain of choosing the easy way out – is long-lasting, and it erodes into our souls. No matter how easy or how hard, the choices you make will decide whether you sleep in peace knowing you tried, or forever suffer sleepless nights of guilt and shame. It takes courage in your soul to stay on track, and to relentlessly pursue your dreams.

There are so many examples of women throughout history who defied the rules of a patriarchal society and who dared to go after their dreams. While many women may have gone uncelebrated, the one who exemplifies this fortitude to pursue her dreams is the renowned scientist Marie Curie, who was awarded the Nobel Prize for her work.

> *"I was taught that the way of progress is neither swift nor easy."*
>
> **– Marie Curie**

## Marie Curie

Born in the era when women's rights were negligible, Marie Curie dreamed of venturing into learning and science, a world forbidden to women. While women were barred from higher education, she did not let the societal norms crush her dreams, and secretly attending the "Flying University," an underground, *illegal* network of classes for women.

Breaking absurd rules designed for women was not her only forte, she also showed great resilience and perseverance. From working menial jobs to living in freezing conditions just to have a roof on her head, she did not let the hardships take away her desire to follow her dreams.

Her work in the fields of physics, chemistry, and mathematics, was looked upon scornfully by territorial men who discounted her contributions to the field. While she and Pierre worked hand in glove, the accolades were only reserved for the male research partner, who also happened to be her husband. Not only did she have to prove herself over and over again, but the award also came to her only after compelling evidence from Pierre himself, to convince the men making these decisions.

Time and again, she was chastised for demanding her rights – the right to do her work and pursue her passion, the right to use her ingenious knowledge to help society, and the right to be recognised for her work. While on one hand, she built and provided x-ray machines for injured men on the war-torn fields, on the other, she stood firmly against the squelching efforts of the men behind the desks. Whether it was standing unapologetically in a room full of male students and teaching them, or walking through the halls filled with disparaging voices, she held her head high as she walked from classrooms to battlefields. She didn't just open doors for herself; she lit the path for other women in science.

We live in a different century, but the norms haven't changed much. While there is loud support for women and their dreams, what transpires behind closed doors on that roundtable full of men is an iniquitous pampering of those large egos. Many dreams are trampled in those rooms under the heaviness of masculine grandeur.

And yet dreams are born.

Throughout the history of mankind, few scientists have made contributions in all three fields of physics, chemistry, and mathematics. The few names that we can count on our fingertips are: Isaac Newton, Marie Curie, Leonardo Da Vinci, Robert Boyle, Michael Faraday, and Henri Poincare. Five men, one woman.

*That* is why her story is so significant – not only because of her research on x-rays, radium, polonium, radiation, and the application of math for radiation and decay, but also because this work was something she had to fight for. If the right to contribute can be denied because of gender, what expectations can we have as we forge our paths towards our goals? The immensity of Marie's fortitude, and the depth of her conviction is beyond our imagination, for her path to success was not an easy one. There are a few lessons that stand out in particular from Marie's life:

### Your dreams come to you from your higher self. Not as a choice but as a purpose.

The purpose of your life comes to you as a strong desire to do something, whether you dream of building an innovative tech solution to save lives, or build a simple solution to help mothers with their children. Whether you write policies that govern ethical use of something or you cook wholesome meals for your family restaurant, whether you teach and motivate young minds or you help the sick find solace. You don't just land on what your purpose is; you have to truly desire it. And when you are lucky enough to have this dream reveal itself to you, it is not just your choice – it somehow becomes your duty to bring it to fruition.

As women, we are gifted with intuition, the art of knowing something to be true. When the universe talks to us through the irrepressible urge to pursue a goal, we know somehow, somewhere in our hearts that we truly need to follow these goals, no matter what anyone tells us. The worry of what could go wrong along the way, or the fear of being crushed by the heat you face, is sometimes enough to abandon the dreams – or change them to suit what others think they should be limited to. We need to remind ourselves that in doing so, we are doing injustice to none other than ourselves.

### Don't make your dreams smaller to fit other people's needs.

When you make your dreams smaller, growth will evade you. Growth, honour, fulfillment, and self-respect will not mean anything to you until you fully commit to your dreams, and until you fully acknowledge that only ice cream comes easy – everything else demands hard work and dedication.

Professional growth will evade you when you don't demand what you need and work for it. You may not think that you are in a race with someone else, because for you it is about your race against time, your race for your own growth. There may be people pitting themselves against you, and winning for them could mean just seeing you lose. When you make your dreams smaller, you are indirectly telling your intuition that you are not ready yet; and telling it to quiet down is going to blind you to the direction and guidance that equals no other.

### Forge your connection with your intuition – it will not just help you identify your goals, it will also guide you along the way.

Men and women have different strengths. For men, it is often their physicality and everything connected to it. For women, it is often their ability to connect to their higher selves and their intuition. While men may be aware of their strength in their physicality, they are woefully unaware – much to our advantage – to the intuitive power of women. Heed this difference, and keep your strengths in mind while looking at your hurdles.

## Let the faith in your strength be larger than the fear of achieving your dreams.

Ignoring these strengths is like cheating yourself by ignoring the ace of spades in your stack of cards– at every struggle, your heart will speak to you, and at every hurdle there is a solution hidden in plain sight. If only you choose to look for the clues, will they reveal themselves. Sometimes the solutions are easy, and most of the time, they will be a key to unlocking your dormant powers. And notice I say the plural of solution – because they always come in multiples, if only we have the eyes to recognize them. There may be just a small test of your integrity, your resilience, and your judgement.

## Break the rules that don't make sense.

The doors to the future are unlocked by those who dare to challenge the redundant. If Marie did not challenge the patriarchy of the time, we would have many a maimed soldier who could not be diagnosed or treated. No future advances in imaging would have been made if she did not bring to humanity the basic ability to see through to the bones with x-rays. What she achieved from her work during her lifetime – money, fame and otherwise – was way smaller than the contribution she made to the field of medicine and science. A lot of courage and sacrifice was demanded by the Universe for seemingly little personal gains; that is the nature of the purpose of life. The outcome may seem too small to you right now, but your contribution and growth may never fully reveal itself to you. Let that not be the deterrent, but instead be the fuel to pursue your dreams. Step into that role, and watch the mystery unfold.

## No one else but you will understand your goals.

You may not find support often in your journey – not because it does not exist, but because you haven't noticed it. When you choose to follow your dreams, you will meet with some resistance. It is undeniable and unavoidable, and in this noise the support is not always clearly evident. Find your tribe, find the right supportive people around you who can be your positive critics and your cheerleaders.

### Don't let isolation lower your spirits.

As they say, the road to the summit is never crowded. You may have companions along the way – some may travel with you for part of the way, and some may join in the journey only to help you through a certain hurdle. While many may surround you early on in the journey, as you rise the crowds will fall. You lose some people along the way; it's the nature of life. As a woman, you can't be insensitive towards these things, and you may want to shed a tear or scream the pain away. As long as you recognize fluidity as the nature of life, though, you will move ahead. Whether it is energy, strength, people or ideas, it will all ebb and flow. As long as the courage within remains, you will move forward. The momentum may vary, the steps may falter, but the movement *will* continue.

### Focus on the voice within, not on the noise outside.

The noise around you may change at times from gossip to criticism or from disapproval to slander. Sometimes the external noise can be loud enough to muffle the voice of the spirit within. Most dreams fail because the noise has completely drowned this inner voice. This is also the Universe's way to filter out the "unripened" dreams from the ones that are ready to be fulfilled. Overcoming the external noise is a proof of commitment to yourself and your dreams. Whether the noise is distracting you early on in your journey, or cropping up at a certain crucial intersection, this noise may be a sharp, annoying background noise, or a constant nagging one, but when your focus is solely on your actions, your goals, and your inner voice, then that noise becomes more like white noise. That is what you must turn it into!

## The Power of Neuroplasticity

There is an additional reason why it is so important to follow your dreams. Right from the early days of evolution, humans have been making slow but definitive strides towards growth and development – it is the core difference between humans and other animals. While the latter only focus on survival and procreation, the former developed a web of information and emotion processing centres in the brain. The homo sapiens developed larger pre-frontal cortex with more complex neurons that control planning, imagination, creativity. The highly sophisticated neurons allowed for empathy and learning by observing others, and the neurons also formed enhanced memory systems that store and analyze massive amounts of complex information – semantic and relational, thereby giving the ability to human beings to observe, analyse and predict patterns, behaviours, and intentions. They used this information early on to communicate, form social connections, trade, build collective cultures, and this eventually led to the formation of large, organized societies.

All of these evolutionary steps took us from being able to create basic sticks-and-stone tools around seven million years ago as homo erectus for rudimentary problem solving and social cooperation. It was only about 600-700,000 years ago that the Homo sapiens evolved into beings with abstract thinking, who used language for communication, and developed symbolic behaviour like early art, building a family, burying of the dead, etc. The creativity and cultural transmission across generations and other social norms were an outcome of this creative human mind that desired safety, stability, growth and community.

In all of this, the most important aspect of the human brain is neuroplasticity. Our brains are highly adaptable to new environments, and as society evolved, so did the difference between man and woman. While a man and a woman are both very different from each other in physical, mental, emotional, and evolutionary perspectives, one commonality between the two is desire- desire for growth and self-preservation.

**Neuroplasticity**

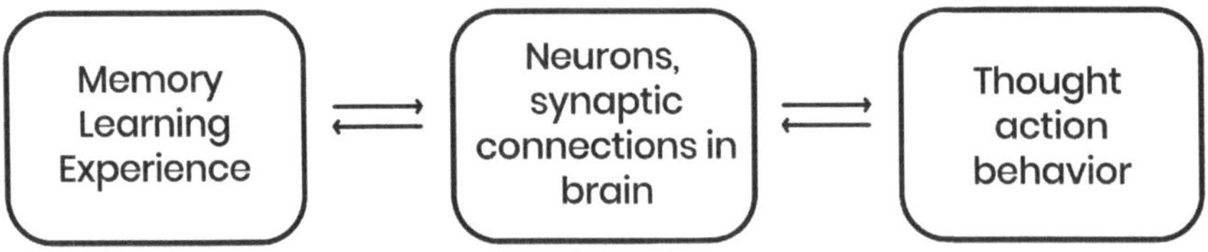


The neuroplasticity of the mind is what presents this desire in different forms in a man and in a woman. While being in the same environment, and exposed to the same threats and dangers, both these brains process the information differently and derive different conclusions. They may have similar goals with a different purpose, or different goals with a similar purpose, but their paths and their journeys will never be the same. A woman, having the core nature of nurturing, caring and inclusion, is different from the territorial and competitive nature of man, and whatever evolution has happened in the last 500,000 years has not been able to change that. Understanding this is the basis of a very important fact.

Your desire to follow your dreams is only natural, and by not listening to your calling, you are ignoring the very core nature of human life. Learn to cross the bridge from your hurdles to your dreams, and do what humans have worked towards for millions of years.

## Taking Action:

If you have already identified your goals, then you may skip steps 1-7 and jump to step 8.

1. **Meditate:** Light a candle. Sit quietly in a cross-legged posture. Focus on your breath. Let the thoughts fade away slowly, keeping your attention on your breath.
2. **Connect with the Universe:** You may call it your higher self, you may call it the Universe, you may call it God. It is now long proven by science that we are not just random beings on this earth; we are a collection of the elements of nature that comprise our body that resides in the ethereal body or the soul. This soul has an imaginary string connecting it to the Higher Self, residing somewhere in Ether. Focus on that connection, focus on that energy.
3. **Express gratitude for this life, for all the blessings.**
4. **Ask the Questions**: *What is my purpose? What am I here to do?*
5. **Focus on Your Breath, Not on Getting the Answer:** The answer may not come to you in the moment – it may be hours, days, weeks, or months.
6. **Take Your Time:** You may sit down for 10 minutes one day, another day for 40.
7. **Sit Down with a Pen and Book:** After you open your eyes, write down everything that comes to your mind. It may not mean anything today, but over the following weeks or months, you will get your answers, and what you write after each session of meditation will slowly begin to reveal something that only has meaning to you.

8. **Write Down Your Goal:** Use clear words, and as much detail as necessary to create a picture of it in your mind. These could be something like "I want to start a business in health and wellness." Or "I want to build SpaceX like fast efficient and reliable transport for global travel" Or it could be " I want to be the CEO of Apple". Make it big, make it bold.

9. **Identify the Reasons:** Write down all the reasons why you should pursue this goal.

10. **Name the Hurdles:** Write down all the things that make you *not* want to pursue this goal. This can include all the hurdles you will face, and can include all external and internal factors, such as any physical, mental, emotional, or financial hurdles that you expect to face or you may already be facing. Give each of these hurdles a rating on a scale of 1-5, with 1 being manageable hurdles to 5 being insurmountable. Also give each hurdle another score, one for the possibility of this happening.

| Hurdles/Problems | Difficulty Levels 1-5 | Probability & Occurrence (1-5) |
|---|---|---|
| | | |
| | | |
| | | |
| | | |
| | | |
| | | |

11. **Take Some Time:** Mulling over the pros and cons of your desires reinforces your conviction *about* your dreams, and makes it easier to manage the hurdles along the way. You may want to spend a few days here before you begin your next steps. You can also occasionally revisit this step.

12. **Map Your Next Steps:** Write down the next five steps towards pursuing your goal. Revisit this list and modify your steps as needed. After you complete your first five steps, then write your next five steps, and so on.

13. **Stay Focused:** Write the reminders for yourself for this journey, such as:

    *"My dreams come to me from my higher self. Not as a choice but as a purpose."*

    *"Don't make my dreams smaller to fit other's needs."*

    *"Forge my connection with my intuition – it will not only help me identify my goals, but will also guide me along the way"*

    *"Let the faith in my strength be larger than the fear of achieving my dreams."*

    *"No one else but I will understand my goals."*

    *"Focus on the voice within, not on the noise outside."*

    *"My desire to follow my dreams is only natural. By not listening to my calling, I am ignoring the very core nature of human life."*

RULE 2

# PICK YOUR BATTLES

Every situation can be turned into a battle, if only you are willing to perish a little with it. Not every war is worth fighting – some battles are just noise, and if you join in, you'll miss the music. They are just distractions, eroding our time and energy.

Imagine a journey where there are no challenges, no conflicts. We traverse the path smoothly, without stress and distraction, and you reach your goal. It's as if time itself slows down for you to be able to accomplish today what you are meant to, so you don't fall behind. The husband and children suddenly turn into divine beings who will do and undo as expected of them, and their schedules will automatically change to suit yours, their expectations will be nil. Maybe even the house gets cleaned and the food gets cooked.

Undoubtedly, *that* would be the journey we all wish for. Walking on a journey towards our dream, having everything fall right into place as if every person around us was placed there to help us reach our goals. Every ounce of organic and inorganic energy or matter aligned in a way to help us build our dream. All the doubt, all the negativities, just fall away. Every person we meet is an angel from up above whose sole purpose is to help us to achieve our biggest, brightest dream. Every situation, every rule, every policy that exists, somehow aligns for us to be able to do this smoothly, with an energy that is unhindered, unperturbed.

Let us muse for a bit and pretend this is all possible, that the Universe turned into your personal genie and granted these wishes to you today, to last until you reach your goal. The happiness, the gratitude, the excitement knows no bounds at receiving such a blessing, and after the initial excitement dies down, the human mind will get to work.

Some may say, *"Well, I don't need all of this, only some part of this will do."* Or some may say, *"I don't need all of this today – just some of these things, some days on demand. Can I wish for this to be true when I wake up in the morning? Can I uber my wishes in? What we expect and what we hope for will change from day to day, so can I have these on demand, ask for something today, something else tomorrow, and even something else day after? Is it really that hard for the Universe to do this for me?"*

After the first few days of having everything work according to you every day, there could be many different directions in which this can go, but the theme will remain the same. The initial contentment to frustration ratio will stay stable for days, weeks, or months, and then slowly but surely start to invert itself. They don't say that the empty mind is a devil's workshop for nothing. Human mind is programmed for problem solving, and when there is not a single problem to solve, the mind gets to work on its second job which it has been programmed for as well – to find problems to solve.

Only a saint can have an empty mind that wanders into the crevices of peace and finds hidden gems of wisdom. For the rest of us, the creative and predictive nature of mind is the source of more than half our problems. Assuming boldly yet humbly that the saintly minds are way ahead in their mindset game, and that they do not need this book at all, I am focusing this conversation on the rest of us. A mind that doesn't have to solve problems and doesn't have to fight challenges will either conjure up *imaginary* problems or will turn you into a demotivated procrastinator with no worry or care in the world. It will either end up developing a "god complex" or it will turn into a monster that finds joy in other people's miseries. In either of these situations, before you know it, it has dragged you miles away from your goals.

**No matter how big or small the struggles appear to be, they can never be bigger than your ability to overcome them.**

Every person actively engaged in this game called life is going to face challenges of some kind, small or big, and each challenge is unique to the individual and their needs or their desires. Some of them come packaged as small inconsequential struggles, some as major life-changing hurdles, but the one secret of the Universe that no one will tell you about is this: It is easy to be swept away in all the challenges and criticism that come your way, but you should not get ruffled by every minor inconvenience. If you fall prey to this urge to expend it on every frivolous skirmish, you will not have enough energy left to focus on what truly matters in building your vision and achieving your goals.

If you're always putting out fires, you won't have the time to build your dreams. Resisting this urge to engage in every battle that you are invited to is not an easy thing to do. It plays on your ego, it plays on your pride, and it so powerfully drags you down the rabbit hole that you can easily lose sight of your goals. Pride is a funny thing – it can expect you to fight, even if the win is a hollow one, and it can come up with innumerable reasons to justify this erosion of your energy.

The challenges you face can be gauged from a few different perspectives, and there are steps to eliminate the unnecessary ones so you can focus on the one battle that you truly have to fight.

The first step is to divide your struggles into the ones that are in your control and the ones that are *not* in your control. Some things can deceptively look like they may be in your control, but things will become more clear over time. These are the kind of challenges that feel extremely urgent to fight, but that if you give them enough time and thought, you will realize that it is an unimpactful and non-consequential fight. This could be things like how people feel about you at your workplace, whether it is your colleagues, your juniors, your managers, or even your employees. It is rarely possible to control how people are going to feel about you, and how they are going to judge you.

I am not saying to be a silent spectator in the process – all I am saying is that whether you like it or not, you are not going to be able to please everyone. There will always be someone that will have a problem with you – how you speak, how you act, what decisions you make, etc. – and you cannot control their perception of you, nor can you control their feelings or their behavior towards you. You cannot control what they say or their motives behind their words. These challenges should be the least of your worries, and yet they often occupy a big place in your mind.

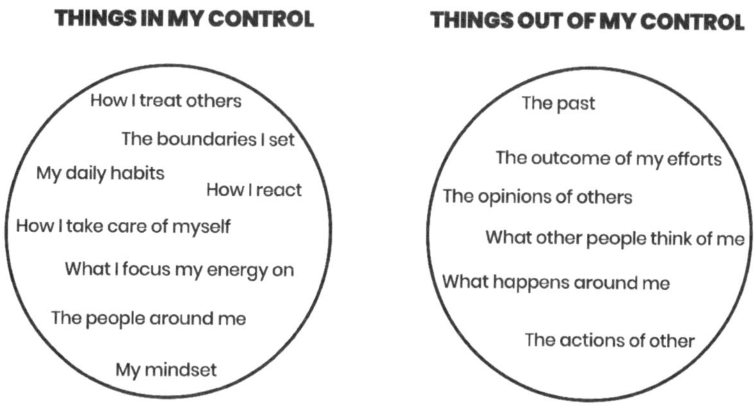


Sometimes the greatest victory comes from walking away with intact self-respect and peace of mind. As women in the workplace, these external "out of my control" challenges are too many to count, but identifying them as trivial and impossible to change spares you a colossal amount of burden and self doubt. Engaging in these kinds of battles takes away your precious time and energy, draining you in small amounts over a long time, like a deep, bleeding wound. The best way is to keep moving forward, engaging in only what is essential.

Things that you can control are: your actions, your feelings, your self-belief, and your attitude towards what comes your way. Put these challenges in "in my control" box. Put the rest in the "out of my control" box and shut the lid tight. This mental act of segregation can be a very powerful tool that helps you allocate your limited resources to the right problems.

* * *

When Hatshepsut took on her royal duty as a woman in 1479 B.C., Egypt was not yet ready for a queen. Her every move, every action was looked upon with suspicion of incompetence. Not only did she still take on that role as a queen, but she also declared herself to be a pharaoh, just like the previous male rulers. She redefined "kingship" and formed alliances with powerful groups that supported her regime, instead of focusing on the distractions from her opponents. She focused on trade and economy, and art and culture, and she engaged the community in building monuments. This allowed her to soften the "out of control" challenges during her lifetime.

Due to the fallacies of the era in which she lived, she was agonizingly aware that those malicious accusations would be redefining her position after she died. History was written by men, and they wrapped women leaders in shrouds of inaccurate descriptions that compared them to the idealist images of women created by men for generations. Any deviation from this idealist image meant that the slandering characterisation was justified.

* * *

Defining your challenges from the ability to control them is the best way to unload a large bulk of them. The next step would be to look at them from the cost vs. benefit perspective.

### Not every battle is yours to fight. There is a price you pay for each one.

When you do decide to fight them, there is always a price to pay, whether it is your time, energy, money, or your peace of mind. Every battle will cost you something, so ask yourself if that price is worth paying. Certain conflicts, in the grand scheme of things, just don't matter. The risk you take, the price you pay for it, and the result that you get, may not make sense at all. These types of challenges are more for the ego or the pride, than to defend the purpose of your life. We don't need to waste our time and energy for battles that do nothing to shorten the distance between us and our goals. Life is short, and even though we may think we have an infinite amount of energy, we have a very finite amount of time, and we can't afford to squander it away on trivialities. It may not be necessary to prove your point every single time. It may not be worth your time to engage in every accusation thrown your way. It is a better idea to sometimes let your actions do the talking. No matter how compelled you feel to prove your point or to prove your worth, allowing time to reveal these facts is a sweet revenge

### Indra Nooyi

As an Indian-born American graduate from Yale School of Management, Indra Nooyi faced many challenges in her navigation of a male-dominated business environment. As a young woman in business, she was constantly undermined in business meetings. In a world where corporate leadership was dominated by men, and women were considered to be too emotional to make business decisions, her suggestions were ignored and later adopted by her male colleagues and seniors, and presented as their own. She experienced microaggressions and was overlooked in corporate settings, her views and opinions ignored and her ability underestimated. She was kept out of informal networks where important business transactions took place, and she also encountered an utter lack of support when dealing with negativities from her male colleagues and supervisors. She also repetitively faced the barriers of gender discrimination and racial bias.

Her story is a story of overcoming barriers with intelligence and perseverance. Nooyi kept herself away from trivial battles and instead let her work do all the talking. She kept her mind clear of the need to fight bias and discrimination and instead focused her time and energy on becoming the best version of herself, as a CEO *and* as a mother. She did not engage herself in trifling arguments with her colleagues, nor did she give in to the urge to prove herself to every coworker who questioned her abilities. Instead, she spent that energy forging strong alliances with the people that mattered.

Sometimes it can take more to walk away than to stand and fight. She often says in her talks that when one door shuts, she doesn't waste time feeling upset with others or feeling sorry for herself, and instead puts her energy towards finding another way in.

Her mindset is clearly visible in her words:

> *"Whatever anybody says or does, assume positive intent. You will be amazed at how your whole approach to a person or problem becomes very different."*

One of Indra Nooyi's key leadership rules is to pick your battles wisely. Her journey is about shattering barriers, not by loud conflicts but by delivering excellence, staying focused, and thinking long term.

* * *

While we focus mostly on which battles *not* to fight, now it's time to look for the ones that you absolutely *must* fight. These are the battles for your values, your principles, and your dreams – these are the battles that will define who you are and what you stand for. These are absolutely non-negotiable.

While we identify our dream and where our passion lies, our core qualities – combined with our grit, our conviction, and our faith – will decide what it is that we stand for. And once you find that, you must defend it with all that you have. Passion can sometimes make us emotional, and if we don't let wisdom lead our passion, it can cost us more than what we can afford. And along the way, the same passion may extinguish. I can't stress the importance of using wisdom, strategy, and good judgement over emotion and ego. And never barter peace for pride – it may seem like a temporary win, but you will ultimately realize the price was not worth paying.

## Cleopatra

As the last active ruler of the Greek-Macedonian Kingdom of Egypt, Cleopatra VII was way beyond the "seductress" myth we read about all the time. Her real secret to success was her intelligence, political instincts, and her ability to adapt in order to overcome her challenges.

Being fully aware of how powerful Rome was, she built strategic alliances with Julius Caesar and Mark Antony. She learned multiple languages and cultures and was able to use diplomacy to turn the tide in favour of Egypt. She used her charm tactfully, and made diplomacy her strongest weapon. The vast amount of knowledge she had about kingdoms, people, languages and cultures, religions, politics, and trade, armed with the discernment of when to get into a battle and when to placate the opponent, made her one of the most brilliant female strategic leaders in history.

Time and again, willingly and tactfully, she lost small battles along the way, to win the war. Her skillful tactics helped her maintain her reign on the kingdom of Egypt and Greece for two decades, and although that may not seem long in today's times, it was a pretty long time for an age where wars, deception, and disease very commonly killed the ruler. This accomplishment of hers has been woefully uncelebrated by historians in comparison to the two-year reign of Julius Caesar.

This is just another classic example of how male historians tend to ignore the strength and accomplishment of female leaders and instead paint them as derogatory and controversial characters.

This distortion of the image of female leaders, whether done with malice or simply mischief, is yet to be analyzed. If we look at society today, whether in movies or at round tables, there is an assumption that if a woman has accomplished as much as or even more than a man, then there is definitely a defect in her character.

And ironically, as women, our goal is to focus on battles that need to be fought, and battles that need to be ignored. While we know that men may not leave a chance at belittling a powerful woman, it is important to not let that distract us, and to instead focus on our goals and what we need to achieve. Giving energy to such out of control matters is going to burn us out.

While sometimes these strategies may be to simply hurt you or vilify you, on a larger impact level, these may be tactics designed to make you take your eyes off the goals. Sheryl Sandberg, the ex-COO of Meta, talks about this in her book, *Lean In*. The best method, as women, to deal with this is to remove emotion from the equation, and simply look at it as a "distract and defeat" method deployed by them. And mind you, men as well as women are equally capable of using this weapon against you.

* * *

This brings us to the next step to identify whether the battle is worth fighting: "What is at risk?"

Unbeknownst to you, the person undermining you the most may be right next to you and may know you extremely well personally and/or professionally. These are very delicate situations and may make you wonder what matters more, the relationship or winning the battle. You can only choose one, because in these situations, winning the battle means losing the relationship. These battles, when they are in a professional setting, put your trust, your support, your camaraderie, and your reputation at risk. In personal relationships, there are other, bigger risks. Keeping the fear, emotions, and disbelief aside, these types of battles need a calm, composed, and factual justification. Overlooking or ignoring these battles may make you feel as if you will be perceived as weak, but know that it is only temporary. It is not an easy decision to step away from these kinds of battles, and it takes a little bit of discipline, wisdom, and self control, and it takes the willingness to let go of the need to always be right.

### Sometimes you let go not because you are weak, but because you choose to be the bigger person.

Remind yourself that the actions of others have nothing to do with who you are, but are instead a reflection of their thoughts, beliefs, and character. Sometimes it is their programming that is miswired, making them insecure and causing them to act out in ways that put your relationship at risk. Can you forgive them? Can you forget? Will they do it again? Are they truly aware of the hurt it caused? Can you trust them again? There are many things to consider. Make your decision wisely.

**Sometimes the battles we choose not to fight set us up for the greatest victories.**

The next step in identifying the worthy battles is to see if they are internal or external. At times, contrary to our belief, we may be jeopardizing our path to success by the battles created in our own heads. The external battles, on the other hand, may or may not be in our control, and that makes us feel very helpless. These battles could range from completely impersonal and impartial (to you) situations like the economy, the geopolitical scenario, a change in policies governing your area of work, or issues somewhat related to you, like your access to resources, support, or finances, the lack of the right team or other personal situations, or factors that other people bring in like their thoughts, ideas, and predatory nature towards you. There could be millions of reasons to feel the stress and pressure of ambition in these situations, but all these extrinsic factors eventually fade when it comes to the impact that arises from internal conflict.

Internal conflict is way more complex and difficult to resolve. What your mind can resolve, your mind can counter; and what your mind can counter, your mind cannot eventually resolve. The human brain is a treacherous landscape – it may start off as a beautiful ideation of a straightforward path, but then randomly, unexpectedly, you will step into the crevices that pull you into the depths of doubts and uncertainty. The beguiling mind keeps you in the dark about the highly deceptive nature of these inner conflicts. Like a cancer that grows inside a body without a single hint for months or years, they breed in silence, growing in size and slowly eating into your strengths. And, like a cancer, sometimes the only way to find these is to screen for them.

Finding these inner weaknesses is a tenuous task, and it consumes some of your willpower and a lot of your precious energy. In an already unpredictable world, it seems like a criminal waste of time and other resources, coupled with the uncertainty and fear of what you would find in that search. But for the wise ones, it's worth the overhaul.

The brutal nature of the inner battles makes it the least of our priorities to deal with. You will always be able to find ways to distract yourself from the urge to face these inner conflicts.

We'd rather live in oblivion, than unveil the mirror. Because it is easy, because it robs us of our ability to blame your failures and your struggles on others. It is discomforting to face your fragility, to identify your vulnerabilities as true. It takes courage to face these head on, fearlessly and without judgement, and to accept and acknowledge what they reveal to you. And for these reasons, they become unattractive enough to not be pursued. When you conquer your inner battles, it makes you stronger than what you have ever known. It is like Popeye's spinach – unappetizing yet powerful!

**In this inner battle, the greatest weapons in your arsenal are brutal honesty and raw courage.**

The truth of the matter is that intrinsic battles decimate you from the inside, whereas the extrinsic battles can be major distractions and command attention. It takes a wise, courageous soul to identify what is crucial. The unveiling of the painful facts can be discouraging, and we may be tempted to give up along the way, to bring our attention back to the outer world, but not giving in to that temptation has serious rewards. Weeding out the inner conflicts, opens up the doors of our outer world as well, as unbelievable as it may sound.

**The rewards may come late, but come, they will.**

> *"The two most powerful warriors are patience and time."*
> **– Leo Tolstoy**

One key principle to picking our battles is the timing of it all. There is a time to speak and time to be silent, there is a time to act and time to wait. When in doubt, resist the impulsiveness and take time to be silent – there is power in this. You may not only walk away as the bigger person; you may also gain valuable knowledge about your opponent and the situation.

While time teaches you how to appropriately respond to these, time also teaches you how to let it all melt away just by adopting a position of mere observer. The thing that differentiates a good argument from a bad one is the timing. It's important to wait for the right time and to approach a conflict with calmness and clarity and not out of impulse. And it's important to also allow yourself the gift of patience, and to let time handle things of its own accord. As Pericles said, "Time is the wisest counselor of all."

Choosing your battles wisely is an act of discernment, and time is your ally. It also brings you clarity of thought, strategic thinking, and resilience – the tools that you will need to fight the rest of your battles. How many times have we been stressed about our problems in the moment, and then casually seen them dissolve in the arms of time? Have you ever wondered why the seemingly big problems suddenly seem to have shrunk and fallen into the sulci of your brain?

## Taking Action:

1. **Create a Chart:** Make a list of things that are "in your control" and "out of your control." Come to this chart every time you face a challenge. Which category does it fall into? If it is an "out of your

control" type of a challenge, it will be easier to let go of, knowing you don't have the power to change it. If its "in your control" type of a challenge, look at your options and make a note of them – but do not act upon them yet.

2. **Take a Moment:** Put this note away for a couple of days and spend time with your family and on other tasks. Even if it seems urgent to act upon. (Unless there is a deadline, in which case, put it away for a couple of hours while you do something else.) The time you take away from this problem and its possible solutions is the time when the Universe gets to work resolving it for you. Sometimes you may notice the problem itself begins to diminish in importance and does not stress you out anymore, or even that it is no longer a battle worth fighting. Sometimes you may come up with a new solution, or one solution may stand out.

3. **Weigh in:** If you take the cue from the universe about whether or not it is your battle or your time to fight, the next step is to weigh in on what you will gain if you win the battle. Is it worth it? What will you lose in return – time, money, energy, peace of mind?

4. **Evaluate Your Relationships:** Next, weigh in is if there is a relationship at stake. Ask yourself what matters more to you – winning this battle or keeping this relationship? Be brutally honest with yourself – don't let your ego and your pride play you. Whether it is personal or professional, how much does this relationship mean to you? Is it possible to resolve the conflict without damaging the relationship, or is it best to walk away from it?

5. **Face Your Fears:** And lastly, after you get an honest answer to that question, ask yourself if the real battle here is internal or external.

Face your inner fears and ask yourself if the battle actually has roots internally or not. If it is internal, find the right tools and right support in loving and trustworthy friends, your spouse, or a family member. If it is external and it is your battle to fight, give yourself some time again, to strategize and let time do its thing. Resist the urge to be impulsive.

## RULE 3

# MAKE TOUGH DECISIONS

The only chance we have at creating our destiny is our ability to make choices. Our choices shape our karma, and our karma shapes our life.

We may let this statement paralyse our thoughts and decision making, or we may let it elate us with excitement at being co-creators of our life – the choice is ours. It is not uncommon to have an initial sense of fear or anxiety at this thought, but letting that fear or anxiety predominate your thoughts and cripple your ability to make decisions undermines your power to determine your future. Because the only way we will ever know if we can achieve something is by taking action – inaction can never cause grief, nor can it cause excitement nor purpose.

*Decision* is a word of Latin origin and French influence, and is made up of the parts "de" – meaning "off" or "away" – and "-cision," meaning to cut off. Like many words adapted from Latin, the word has an implied meaning. Decision literally means "to cut off" all other options, to eliminate all other choices or discussions or arguments, and to come to a conclusion about something.

We are faced with innumerable decisions in our day to day lives – some big, some small, some crucial, some inconsequential, some life-changing. Physiologically speaking, while the prefrontal cortex (PFC) and the limbic system are the primary areas involved in this process, the brain also utilizes a much more complex network of neurons for decision-making.

The prefrontal cortex is the logical department, which uses its working memory, evaluates the options at hand, the risks and benefits of each decision, and makes choices based on experience and goals. It essentially creates a working memory based on the data at hand while making logical interpretations.

The limbic department, on the other hand, is full of emotional employees. The amygdala is responsible for the fight or flight response, fear, anxiety, uncertainty, etc., and it tends to attach emotional significance to every piece of logical information. The hippocampus, on the other hand, is like a database of memories – mostly real, sometimes perceived – based on the type of emotional state while the filing was happening. It also creates memories on the go by merging and segregating these files, poking the amygdala along the way, just for fun.

These different departments go back and forth, presenting their arguments, until a clear winner is found and the decision is made. The orbitofrontal cortex and the ventromedial cortex act as the moral police, or more precisely control the ethical department. where values and principles are determined.

**Decision-making pathway in men**

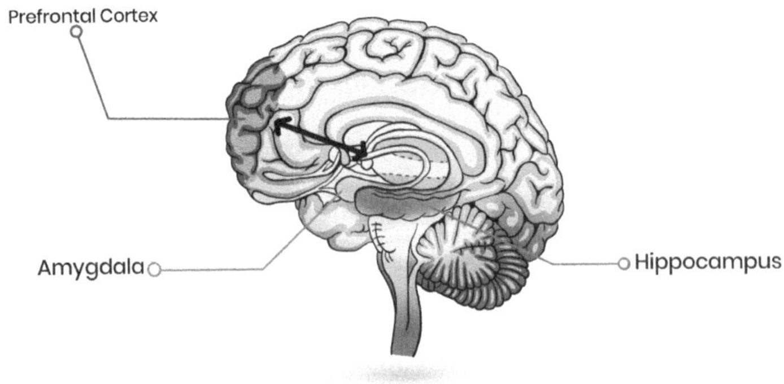

The only difference between AI and humans is that AI will do this loop until it arrives at a conclusion. In humans, however, the loop goes on – even after the decision has been made, it's a never-ending roller coaster. The biggest challenge for cognitive neuroscience is to relate the incredibly complex behavior of humans to the equally complex activity of their brains. No amount of research has bridged this gap between neural activity and biological function.

*"May your choices reflect your hopes, not your fears."*

**– Nelson Mandela**

## The Brain and Hormones

The male brain usually tends to make decisions faster, though not particularly because of any evolutionary advantage over women. Science has come to understand the gender-based differences in evolution, and in this case, the male brain has adapted to silence the emotional ramblings of the limbic system, and has the ability to bribe the ethical department of the orbitofrontal and the ventromedial cortices. They are programmed with the default supposition that their decision is the right one to make, and the pathway from information to interpretation to decision is a pretty straightforward, emotionless journey, unless of course the decision to be made is a personal one and extremely important to their personal relationships.

Women on the other hand, are more complex in their thought process. First, the ethical department has way more power and is constantly demarcating black from white, un-doables from doables. While this can be perceived as a positive as well as a negative trait, depending on the context, it is an essential trait that serves us in times of doubt and uncertainty. Secondly, the limbic system is way mightier than that in men. Studies have shown that women tend to have a relatively larger and more active limbic system, particularly in regions such as the orbitofrontal cortex and parts of the amygdala, which correlates with increased emotional processing and higher regulation capabilities.

**Decision-making pathway in women**

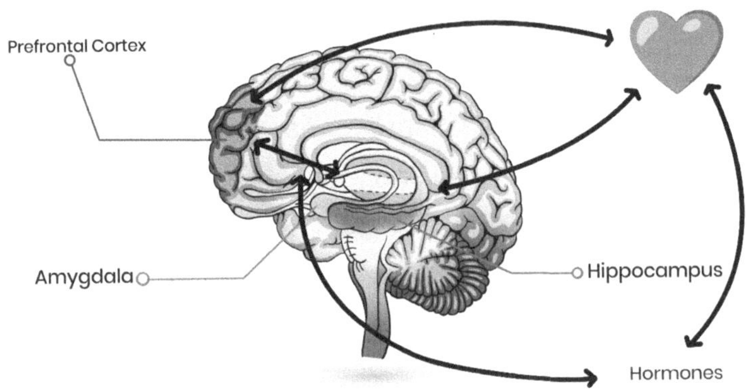


The number of thoughts, emotions, feelings, memories the female brain processes per second is way higher than a masculine brain, presumably due to the size and density of the neural network in these parts of the brain. A large meta-analysis published in *Neuroscience & Biobehavioral Reviews* (2014) by Ruigrok et al. found that women generally have a robust neuronal network in the limbic system. This not only explains sex-based differences in the decision-making process, but also ties into the differences in reactivity to certain situations in life.

Now add to a blend of hormones in that ebb and flow with the cycles of the moon. Estrogen increases amygdala reactivity, especially during the follicular phase leading up to ovulation, and this heightened reactivity can enhance emotional sensitivity, especially to social and emotional stimuli. Estrogen also enhances neuroplasticity and neurogenesis in the hippocampus, which may lead to better memory formation and recall during the ovulatory phase.

In contrast, progesterone, which rises in the luteal phase, may reduce hippocampal activity and connectivity, which could affect mood and memory. Functional MRI studies (e.g.,, Dreher et al., 2007; Petersen et al., 2014) show that limbic-prefrontal connectivity changes during the cycle – for example, during high-progesterone phases, there may be less top-down regulation of the amygdala by the prefrontal cortex, which might lead to greater emotional lability or vulnerability to stress.

And if this wasn't enough, we are blessed with another centre of emotion – the heart. Each decision that passes through the complex pathways of the brain and gets approved has to pass through the final approval from this boss. This particular centre of decision making is quite an unpredictable, and often fallible. Sometimes this centre overhauls all the logical interpretations of the prefrontal cortex; at other times, when it seems impossible *to get over* the emotional narrative of the limbic system, or the baseless fears and worst-case scenarios conjured up by mixing innumerable data and memory files, the decision is made by the valorous little heart. However, it does not ignore every idea, every suggestion from the brain – it may sometimes do that in personal relationships, but always, this heart will function hand in glove with the ethical department of the orbitofrontal cortex and the ventromedial cortex. Initially it may speak softly, but if the boss has decided to take the plunge, those mutters then become a loud proclamation.

> *"Truly successful decision-making relies on a balance between deliberate and instinctive thinking."*
>
> **– Malcolm Gladwell**

This may have felt like too much scientific lingo and you may have been tempted to skip to the next part of the chapter, but having an awareness about the physiology of decision making, is key to freeing yourself from the false belief that you are too weak to be able to make tough decisions. The complexity of thought and decision in a woman's psyche is unfathomable. While society makes us see it as a weakness, it is actually an undeniable power to have so many more influences in our decision-making process. With it, the possibilities are endless.

### Indira Gandhi

One woman, who is known to have aced the art of decision-making is Indira Gandhi, India's first and only female prime minister (1966–77, 1980–84) – she was both admired and feared for her decisiveness. Many of her decisions centralized power and pushed India toward a more state-controlled model, while others strengthened national security and sovereignty. Her legacy remains unparalleled, and her fearless, visionary leadership and decision-making ability was hailed by some and criticized by others. Globally and in India, she was both praised and criticized and was often labeled authoritarian.

Whether it was a decision to declare a nationwide state of emergency in 1975, or to conduct a bold security action against Sikh militants inside the Golden Temple, a sacred religious site, she faced choices that were polarizing and damaging to her reputation. While she may have made decisions based on economic growth and national security, the aftermath of these decisions was brutally damaging and eventually proved to be fatal for her.

She nationalized major commercial banks to increase credit access for rural and priority sectors, and did not fear going against the business elite and the corruption of her own political party. She also made the high-stakes decision to support the Bengali nationalist movement in East Pakistan, which culminated in India's military intervention and the Indo-Pakistani War of 1971. While many innocents died in that war, the decision of supporting East Pakistan was as much of a strategic decision as a needs-based decision in post-partition India.

> *"Nothing is more difficult, and therefore more precious, than to be able to decide."*
>
> **– Napoleon Bonaparte**

Under her leadership, India conducted its first nuclear test in 1974. The test, named "Operation Smiling Buddha," marked India's entry into the nuclear club. The decision to pursue nuclear weapons was another example of her prioritizing national security over the feelings of western nations, which then sanctioned India. While her stand was that it was a peaceful nuclear testing, it was in a way, a flexing of muscles to deter India's hostile neighbors. Her decisions not only achieved that with flair, but also instilled a sense of national pride amongst the masses. She was a pioneer in laying down the foundation for India's future nuclear standpoint.

While her choices and her decisions may not have found support in the international or the domestic community, it reinforced her position as a firm, decisive and influential leader.

### The price you had to pay for a decisive action, shrinks in time in comparison with the significance of that action.

Throughout history, women have rarely been given the right to make big decisions, and are often disliked for the decisions they made.

Indra Nooyi, the former CEO of PepsiCo, faced the fear of being disliked by her colleagues, and yet drove the company towards including healthy food like Quaker Oats, while also never going too far from the original mission and products of the company. She restructured the company's product portfolio to carry "healthy for you," "good for you," and "fun for you" categories of food and drinks. It was only after the success of that bold decision that she was given the position of CEO.

## Ginni Romety

Another such leader whose strong resolve and timely decisions impacted the course of a company was Ginni Romety from IBM. She was the first woman to head IBM in its over 100-year history, and she led the company through a profound strategic pivot – from legacy hardware and services to cloud computing, AI, and data analytics. As the chairwoman, president, and CEO of IBM, there was never a dearth of tough decisions to be made.

> *"You may not control all the events that happen to you, but you can decide not to be reduced by them."*
>
> **– Maya Angelou**

Her strong personality and tough decision-making changed the course of IBM and her broader legacy in the world of business. Her bold, transformative leadership, and her strong belief in proactive reinvention were the keys to her success. "Growth and comfort do not coexist," is a mantra she has often shared. Her resilience gave her the ability to take bold strategic risks in the face of internal team and investor skepticism, especially with major acquisitions and long-term bets on emerging tech.

Against internal resistance, she made the decision to pivot to hybrid cloud computing with the $34 billion acquisition of Red Hat in 2018 – at the time, one of the largest software acquisitions. She acted on her firm belief that the industry is heading towards open-source software and AI, and she changed the trajectory of IBM. Her decisions divested IBM from high-risk, low-margin commodity (PC and IT infrastructure services) to high-risk, high-margin innovative sectors of AI, cloud computing, quantum computing, and cybersecurity. Though her path was difficult, her resolve and her vision were enough to drive her and to empower her to make tough decisions.

During her tenure in IBM, and even later on, through her work in employee reskilling programs in AI and digital tech, she has helped redefine corporate learning and workforce development globally. She pioneered the transformation of IBM's culture from rigidly hierarchical to more agile and innovative, and thereby turned into a role model for women in global enterprise leadership.

While today Nooyi and Romety are hailed as innovative and influential leaders, leading change and transformation in the corporate world, the decisions they made and the backlash they faced during the decision making process was not an easy one. That did not deter them, but rather, solidified their resolve.

> *"Sometimes you make the right decision, sometimes you make the decision right."*
> **– Phil McGraw**

## Every decision you make is a reflection of who you are.

Irrespective of the field that you are in, you will be required to make tough decisions. Sometimes it is easy, and sometimes it feels too exhausting or too risky to have to do that. If you are a business owner, or in a position where you are responsible for making decisions that are relevant to the success or failure of the company, it becomes even more tiring, as the decisions to be made seem endless.

As women, we have hundreds of decisions to make daily, at work and at home – decisions with our colleagues and supervisors or with our spouse, decisions involving employees or involving our children, decisions about business or about the kitchen, decisions about strategy and marketing or those about a social evening with friends.

Decision fatigue is a real thing, and the first step we can do to prevent this is to eliminate all the "not necessary for me to choose" choices from our day. Take help from your husband and your children and let them take over some of the home decisions, like what to eat, where to go, what the weekend looks like, which sports to enroll in, which movie to watch on Friday night, which games to play on a game night, which restaurant to go to on a date night, etc.

It shouldn't be surprising that even such small decisions lead to fatigue and a lack of desire to procrastinate or avoid making important decisions.

> *"Decision is a sharp knife that cuts clean and straight; indecision, a dull one that hacks and tears and leaves ragged edges behind it."*
>
> **– Gordon Graham**

Another way to avoid decision fatigue is to avoid making important decisions in the evening, at the end of a long busy day. Most decisions made then are influenced not only by decision fatigue but also by the small frustrations or bits of rage and disappointment, which collect to form a large ball of negative emotions in our heads. It would be ideal to wait until morning to make important decisions – time itself can come to our rescue and allow us to analyse the situation at hand with a fresh new perspective. Sometimes delaying – but not avoiding – decision making until the right time has its own benefits.

> *"It is often said that a wrong decision taken at the right time is better than a right decision taken at the wrong time."*
>
> **– Pearl Zhu**

Sometimes decision fatigue comes from having *too many* choices. This is known as paradox of choice. Do not let too many choices fumble you on your path. If we narrow it down to two options at a time and keep eliminating the options, we will eventually arrive at a much smaller number of choices, perhaps two or three. Our brain functions a lot more efficiently when we can focus and evaluate something mindfully, instead of being clouded by a million thoughts. Beyond a point, a larger number of irrelevant thoughts conjoin into a negative ball of emotions, and narrowing it down to a smaller number of options makes the decision-making process less overwhelming.

> *"A decision made from fear is always the wrong decision."*
>
> **– Tony Robbins**

Whenever you're confronted with different choices, you must first ask yourself if they will get you closer to your goals or farther away. If the answer is closer, then pull the trigger. If it's farther away, make a different choice. Sometimes the question at hand may not give you clarity about this – if so, ask yourself which choice favours the greater good of the business, or aligns with your purpose and make decisions accordingly. Conscious choice making is a critical step in the success of your dreams and your business.

One of the questions that paralyzes us is the fear of making the *right* choice. We fear how people will perceive us when we make that choice. We worry about failure. We worry about being labeled as authoritative, too pushy, too weak, or of poor judgement. We worry about hurting others or getting in the bad books of our co-workers, and we worry about being labeled heartless or inexperienced.

Indira Gandhi, as we saw above, was widely condemned as being authoritarian and was accused of human rights violations. She was also called out for damaging India's democratic institutions and earned bad reputation for her strong, unwavering decisiveness. She only focused on the big questions at hand, however, and ultimately made difficult choices that brought economic discipline, industrial efficiency, and a surge in national pride. Her role in putting India on the world map as an emerging regional power and a nuclear capable state is undeniable. She didn't always make the right choices, but she made the choices nevertheless according to her idea of the nation. She may have made poor choices along the way, but instead of bogging herself down with self-deprecation, she changed paths as needed and made better ones.

> *"Don't mourn over your bad decisions. Just start overcoming them with good ones."*
>
> **– Joyce Meyer**

Similarly, Ginni Romety did not shy away from tough decisions. While some of her decisions were transformational for IBM, some of them were crucial in shaping the workforce all over the country and even globally. She made decisions and stood by them, which earned her recognition during her stint at IBM, as well as new avenues when she left.

> *"Choices are the hinges of destiny."*
>
> **– Pythagoras**

We all face difficult life decisions, either in the professional or the personal space of our lives, and the worry of being wrong is a powerful deterrent. If this fear is holding you, then we need to zoom out a little and give ourselves a broader perspective.

Renowned psychologist Dr Jordan Peterson has a very unique way of analyzing and interpreting the human psyche in a given situation. He says that, "When you're thinking about what is going to go wrong if you make the wrong choice, also remind yourself, what could go wrong if you don't make a choice at all…Sometimes the cost of not making a decision is far worse than the cost of making a wrong decision, even if the decision is risky."

One way for our brain to protect its sanctity is to avoid making decisions – zero choice, zero anxiety. This is true for major life-changing decisions – when faced with these, it is crucial to weigh the risks and benefits of each of the options in front of us, as well as the risks and benefits of *not* doing anything. Right or wrong, the option we pick puts us in a way better position than completely forgoing the choices. Many let go of this power to choose and find themselves stuck in the same situation, same job, same position, same issues and same cycle for years, leading to a feeling of dissatisfaction and void in their lives. It's a hard reckoning that by not making the choices, we lose way more than what we are prepared for in the long run.

**No two people will face the same challenges even while being on the same path, because while the paths are the same, the journey is different.**

We are always faced by choices, and these choices shape our future and our destiny. Either of the paths we choose, is filled with plentiful of struggles and challenges of their own. One path may seem more easy or straightforward, one a little windy with obviously perceivable challenges. But the matter of fact is that each of these paths will have challenges, hidden or obvious, small or big, short term or long lasting, trifling or life changing. Another fact is that no two people will face the same challenges even while being on the same path, because while the paths are the same, the journey is different. It is the Universe's way to hone our character, to test our fortitude and to build our resilience. That is the crux of evolution – evolution of Self, and evolution of Universe.

> *"It is in your moments of decision that your destiny is shaped."*
> **– Tony Robbins**

Having an open mind and conceding to this ancient wisdom about humanity and evolution, rids us of the need to be liked by all. Our journey is for no one else to understand, and our perspective is unique to us. How we think about a problem, and what we think of as a solution, may not be clearly visible to everyone around us immediately. And that is ok. Our decisions must match our values and principles, and as long as we are able to sleep at night, or look ourselves in the mirror without shame or regret, it is the right decision.

## Make your decision and stand by it.

Once we get over the hunch of indecisiveness, the next hurdle is regret. Regret is a funny thing, and is another one of those capabilities that comes as a result of being an analytical animal. We tend to doubt or question our decisions even after making them. We question ourselves repeatedly about the validity and the correctness of our decision, and in doing so, we are presuming that "other choice" that we did not take would've been the better one. This is one of the biggest disadvantages of human imagination – we can imagine the catastrophes of our choice, not just before but even *after* making a decision. Understanding the worst-case scenarios early on and being mentally prepared for such a consequence not only helps us stay on track, but over time, it also reveals the ways to overcome these consequences.

No one is infallible, and irrespective of our best intentions, we will make mistakes. Let those mistakes lead to learning, not paralyzing future decision making.

> *"Great leaders don't lead others with bitterness or resentfulness of past mistakes – they lead with hope and knowledge of the past to inform greater decision making in the future."*
>
> **– Spencer Fraseur**

> *"The future is fluid. Each act, each decision, and each development creates new possibilities and eliminates others. The future is ours to direct."*
>
> **– Jacque Fresco**

## Taking Action:

1. **Proactively Avoid Decision Fatigue:** Outsource all inconsequential decision making to your spouse, family or co-workers.
2. **Stay Calm:** When you are faced with a major life changing decision, stay calm. Give yourself some time to overcome the initial anxiety related to the situation. If possible, sleep on it.
3. **Bedtime Meditation:** Express gratitude for your life, your family, fulfilling career, etc. Express gratitude to the Universe or to God for being there for you in times of need. Focus on your breath, and mentally visualize the problem or question at hand. Avoid the urge to look for a solution or to evaluate your options, and instead jump ahead – picture yourself having made the decisions you needed to make, and see yourself reaping the benefits of the outcome that you are expecting. Request that Universe or God help you to get there, then go to sleep.
4. **Take Notes:** If you wake up with a decision, or some ideas around the decision, make notes of your thoughts, including all the pros and cons of that choice. If you don't already have a clear winner yet, you will at least have some clarity of thought. You may also want to simultaneously make a note about the pros and cons of *not* making a decision in the given scenario.
5. **Examine the Worst-Case Scenario:** Write down or chart out the possible negative outcomes for each of the choices, whether you make them or you don't make them. Not being OK with certain outcomes will eliminate some of your options and make decision making a little bit easier. Consider the worst-case scenarios in each of these situations and eliminate some more choices.

6. **Explore Risks and Benefits:** From the remaining options, weigh in the risks and benefits, looking at each one of them through the lens of your values and principles. Which decision will *not* disrupt your peace of mind, and let you sleep peacefully at night? Which decision will allow you to look yourself in the eye without guilt?
7. **Seek Counsel:** If there is still any doubt, see an advisor who has your back, someone who has a neutral perspective. If it is a decision that impacts your family, you'll want to counsel with your partner.
8. **Stick to Your Decision:** Stick to your decision and avoid regret. Remind yourself of the greater picture, and avoid self doubt.

RULE 4

# LET YOUR ACTIONS SPEAK LOUDER

People will look at you the way you look at yourself – *you* decide how good you want their vision to be. Being confident in your own skin is a hard skill to build, but once you do that and truly get comfortable with who you are, the world is your oyster.

Imagine a boardroom table, an important corporate meeting. Person A has an assertive voice, firm tone, and an air of confidence about them. Their body language is open, bold, and dominating. Their opinions may or may not be excellent but their confidence is unwavering.

Person B, on the other hand, has a quiet low voice, and expresses a bold new innovative idea to deal with the situation. But their body language is timid – they may be sitting on the edge of their chair or having a nervous smile on their face.

Now what did you imagine? Did you imagine person A as a male and person B as a female? More than 90% of us reading this will have imagined it this way.

*"Believe in yourself! Have faith in your abilities! Without a humble but reasonable confidence in your own powers, you cannot be successful or happy."*

**– Norman Vincent Peale**

Even after years of being in the workforce, and years of successful careers and businesses, women still often feel compelled to prove their every action, decision, win, and loss.

The need to prove ourselves as women comes from many different factors – external as well as internal – and we need the four Cs to avoid getting caught in these repetitive behaviors. The four Cs are **Calm, Confidence, Clarity, and Communication**. And while most of this problem originates outside of us, the solution is actually found *within* us. The source of the problem may be in the thoughts, words, or actions of others, but it is an "out of control" problem. Subconsciously, however much we avoid brooding on it or engaging with, these battles play on our self-esteem and on how we show up. So we try to prove ourselves every step of the way. We must let go of that need to prove ourselves, and we do so by going inwards and looking for ways to empower ourselves.

*"Public opinion is a weak tyrant compared with our own private opinion."*

**– Henry David Thoreau**

## Calm

The first sign of courage is calmness in the face of adversity. In our work environments, just like in the other areas of life, there is a trend that we have observed, possibly due to the mindset brought by the newer generations for their sense of ego and satisfaction. The other possibility is that the older generations have promoted this mindset, knowing that they have raised a sensitive generation. I call it the paradox of niceness.

We usually see people of different talents and capabilities in the workplace, and with varying levels of quality of these traits. Every person has the right to have the opportunity to prove themselves, to work hard, and to earn a living and a good reputation. The culture of inclusiveness provides everyone this opportunity; however, an excess of anything is never good. How does it make you feel when an average- or a low-performing employee gets a "nice job," "good job," or "keep it up" from their colleagues or managers? Or when, on the other hand, a highly productive and brilliant employee comes up with a great idea in a meeting and is dismissed? The paradox of niceness is real.

Niceness culture can be overly exaggerated. In an attempt to be sensitive towards others' feelings, we have bred a culture that encourages mediocrity and rewards it beyond measure, to the extent that the more mediocre you are, the lower the chance that you will ever be shown the mirror. The criticism is reserved for the more productive ones, for every small mistake they make.

It is likely that this niceness culture brewed at homes and at schools and playgrounds before it entered workplace culture. The millennials raised their kids with "good job" for every small thing that they did, even normal human things like walking or talking or being kind or hitting the ball. It has reached a point where dancing asynchronously on stage even in a small team for what was supposed to be a coordinated dance, to doing taekwondo with zero force and only soft unpurposeful hand movements and poor posture, are also rewarded with a similar "great job". This superfluous positive reinforcement has instilled a sense of unerring self and false self esteem. While saying "good job" or "great job" is not wrong, what's wrong is how frequently it is being said to young minds these days. From the overzealous parents to the "appropriateness" in the school culture, children are sent through a continuum of false positive reinforcements. The niceness culture is rooted deep in our society – taking away grades and ranks and replacing them with arbitrary adjectives to make children feel equal and not pressured, providing children with fidgeting toys to keep them in the class and ignoring discipline, dumbing down math to an extent that it eliminates the need for critical thinking, making solving math questions way more lengthy and complex, denying social interactions at lunchtime and replacing them with Disney movies, ignoring the need for challenge and focusing on bringing everyone down to the weakest capabilities in the class, and focusing on people pleasing skills and feelings rather than facts and critical thinking and learning. The niceness culture has rooted itself deeply in our society.

The same children then grow up and enter into the workforce expecting the same culture of mediocrity. The more hard-working, efficient colleagues are supposed to be more resilient and more tolerant of our critique, so we burden them with negative feedback arising from the misgivings of those and others.

If you are being criticized or questioned for the decisions that you have made, or the success that you have achieved, know that it is not you. It is the paradox of niceness that makes people bring out these expressions – so let it not become the force that takes you down the barrage of explanations in order to prove yourself. Not every action or every decision can be justified from a bigger strategy perspective, but at the same time, whether the decision was big or small, each person will think, act, and function differently, based on the situation, as well as their knowledge, experience, maturity, understanding and resilience.

One's risk-taking ability is another major factor that influences decision-making. Some facts and some numbers can be justified, but if you try to prove yourself all the time, it will be an exhaustive circle of "decision explanation" from which you can never escape.

The most important strategy to be calm. Not all questions raised to your face need to be answered – some of them are rhetorical questions, and some of them are derogatory comments posed as questions. The best way to answer these is with silence. Pause. Breathe. Stay calm.

Let the inappropriate comments or questions fall into the gap created by the silence. Pauses invoke trust and intrigue from the other person, and sometimes even introspection about their own words. The pause and the breath will bring the centre of your energy inwards, and it will help you stay distant from the emotional impact of the question, preventing you from taking things too personally. Once that calm grounded energy has taken over, the need to give any explanation will automatically dissolve. What direction the conversation goes from thereon is fully in your control, and not a reaction to a perceived blame or a threat.

> *"She remembered who she was and the game changed."*
> **– Lalah Delia**

In all of this, one thing that is crucial, is to stop giving ourselves the impossible task of being perfect. If we only aim for perfection, we are setting ourselves up for failure, as that is a target that is ever elusive. After years of experience pursuing this exact same goal, if we haven't learnt that yet, we are our own biggest enemies. Even before someone says something, we will be prepared in our minds to accept and defend the "not so perfect" decision.

Perfection is a mirage we will never be able to reach. Once we understand that there is no perfect decision, the way we look at ourselves changes. Doing the calm breathwork and energy will help us stay focused, and the breath will prevent our fight or flight response from taking over – and will get us out of explanation mode.

> *"If you have no confidence in self, you are twice defeated in the race of life. With confidence, you have won even before you have started."*
> **– Cicero**

## Confidence

Confidence is about how we feel and how we show up. It's about how we express ourselves in uncomfortable situations. It is not just about what we know, but also about what we *don't* know and being comfortable in the absence of that perfection.

Confidence begets clarity and clarity begets confidence, and they are both so intertwined that you need to have a little bit of both to even get started. To have the clarity to understand that confidence will actually *bring* more clarity into our actions and our decisions, and to have the confidence to turn inward to get more clarity about our thoughts, purpose and goals, are two sides of the same coin.

While we explore clarity a little bit later, let's bring our focus to confidence. Confidence is born from having the courage to be disliked. That does not mean that we *want* to be disliked; that is not the purpose of the confidence. It is that we are okay with being disliked for our dreams and for our actions. It is the desire to be recognized that makes us inadvertently attached to other people's opinion of us. To get free from the clutch of these non-complementary relationships, confidence is key.

*"To overcome fear is the quickest way to gain your self-confidence."*

**– Roy T. Bennett**

Confidence may sometimes be visible in our posture, or the superwoman stance, in the way we make eye contact or in the way we dress to kill. Sometimes it is more subtle, and only shows up in critical situations, such as in the silence before the words come out, in thc ability to say no, or in the ability to shrug off contempt or condescending comments. Whether we show the obvious signs of confidence or carry the more subtle ones, it is a reflection of the true culmination of being comfortable in your skin. It is the sign of a secure woman, one who does not seek validation from anyone, but one who functions with a quiet conviction.

It is something that allows us to stand alone and not be afraid of it, and in doing so breed more confidence. This confidence makes us distant from the need for validation, and the need to prove our worth every step of the way.

All of us humans are born with a finite amount of time and a finite amount of energy, and how well we utilize these finite resources to fulfill the purpose of our lives will determine whether we succeed or not. Confidence is the booster of these finite resources.

How can we foster confidence in a world where people around us want us to fail? It is not always an easy task, but how you show up is the first sign of your confidence. Being confident, even on days when you don't feel so, requires changing focus from one part of our being to another. While confidence is very much an internal feeling, it can be fuelled by external assistance. Dress to kill and step into those heels and half the battle is ours.

There are innumerable factors like our hormones that make us feel physically and mentally "not up to it." Maybe your bestie is going through a tough time, or your child is dealing with a bully at school, or one of your parents is unwell, or maybe your nanny did not show up and you have an important presentation, or you are feeling the pains of perimenopause. There are always reasons to ditch the confidence. But actually these are the reasons to hold on to the confidence all the more. How we choose to stand or sit in the meeting matters. The physical feedback loop of confidence lies in erect spine, open broad shoulders, and noticing yourself connected to the ground underneath your feet. And in virtual meetings, what can help boost confidence is a standing desk with a walking pad.

> *"Life is either a daring adventure or nothing at all."*
>
> **–Helen Keller**

After we conquer the physical gesture and body language of confidence, we need to ace the vocal and verbal signs of confidence, which are speaking in an audible (medium loud, no muttering) and assertive tone of voice. Speaking with a slow pace, a clear separation of words, a natural flow of sentences, and strategic, emphatic pauses. Then add a confident smile and make eye contact as we speak. Just these small steps can add a truckload of confidence to how you show up, regardless of the feeling you started out with.

A few things to proactively avoid are fidgeting, distracted eyes, playing with your hair, whispering or muttering, or using a monotonous voice. While we may not be able to control how our physiology reacts to how we're feeling – a fast heart rate, a slight rise or dip in blood pressure leading to tiny beads of sweat in our palms or on our forehead, shallow breath, or a quiver in the voice – any symptoms may be giveaways of anxiety or anticipation. Breathing slow and deep can come to our rescue again, as it drowns away the fight or flight response and calms the nerves.

For some it is easy, but for others confidence comes with practice-practice with the purpose of tapping into our authentic selves. As obnoxious as it may sound, recording ourselves and watching the videos can be helpful, as we can look for signs of confidence and signs of anxiety, and then work on them, daily or otherwise. This is a great way to not only learn by observing, but also as a way to record progress.

> *"No one can make you feel inferior without your consent."*
>
> **–Eleanor Roosevelt**

## Clarity

There are certain human facts, and understanding these facts gives us immense clarity into how we can operate in the cutthroat world, build a fulfilling career and accomplish the purpose of our lives. Here they are:

- Our time and energy are finite. We can either squander it by needing to prove our worth, exhaust these resources along the way, or we can use them wisely to traverse our path at a steady pace.
- Confidence is intrinsic, but it can also be a learned behavior. On days that you are more confident, go ahead and conquer the world, but on the days when you have difficulty locating it, borrow it from your closet, your prayer room, your meditation room, or your gym.
- There are many physical, vocal, and verbal signs of confidence. Practice to purposefully integrate these into your being.
- They're out to judge us, but that only matters to us if we do something to inject life into their judgement.
- You don't have to show your worth; it is evident for those who want to see it.
- Insecurities are loud, and confidence is quiet. There is no need to say too much about everything to make people believe in your capabilities. You have nothing to prove!
- While someone's initial reaction to your action may be disdain or jealousy, people are actually attracted to confident people – but in either case, they'll say you're a bitch.

> *"Envy comes from people's ignorance of, or lack of belief in, their own gifts."*
>
> **– Jean Vanier**

## Communication

It's not always about what we say – it is also about how we say it. The significance of a silent happy pause, to tap into that confidence and the grounding calm energy, cannot be stressed enough. The pause creates a barrier between the condescending comments or questions and our response, allowing our psyche to eliminate the emotion and keep the facts intact. It sets a tone of intrigue and wonder, and permits us to set the pace of our words, the tone of our voice, and the nature of the response.

Jefferson Fisher, an American lawyer and author of the book *The Next Conversation*, highlights methods of effective communication. He stresses the value of choosing when to speak, and when to let the silence be the chosen response. When it comes to speaking, he says less is more – a person who talks less always gives a greater aura of power than one who talks more.

The most relevant advice in his book is about letting your breath be your first word. Notice how the most powerful people in the world limit their conversations, opinions, and ideas to a few words. In the age of social media, speaking in fewer words may seem counterintuitive, but Fisher observes that the more words it takes to tell a truth, the more they sound like a lie. The more you have to explain something, the less it invokes trust from people about what you are really capable of. So speak relevant stuff using fewer words, because when you are just yapping away, the cause becomes lost in the puddle of words. There is wisdom in only speaking as much as truly relevant.

When we do choose to use the art of communication, we need to remember the basics of doing so effectively. We should use fewer and more effective words, articulate our sentences well, and, most importantly, eliminate filler words – the "um"s and the "ah"s, and "just"s and "I'm sorry to bother you but…"s.

Over apologizing not only puts you in a lower self esteem category in front of the other person, but it also makes them think that you feel unworthy of their time or assistance. Once you overcome this hurdle, the next one is to stop focusing on people pleasing. Be firm and assertive in your communication and use confident language that is not looking for approval and not asking for other people's opinions.

Controlled and well-thought-out words go a long way in building trustworthy relationships and maintaining them. Arguments, or reacting impulsively to other people's opinions of you is not worth your time and energy. It is but a rock in your path, and it is best to walk around it instead of trying to break through it.

In a difficult conversation that may feel more like a trap, it's best to ask questions instead of answering them. Stop reacting to people's interpretations or observations, and resist the urge to argue or explain. Instead, gently and slowly turn the questions at them. Show a genuine interest in what you hear in their responses and try to identify their intent. Instead of giving them the satisfaction of playing with your emotions, use assertiveness or humour to set boundaries.

Sometimes a confrontation may be unavoidable, and for many of us, it can be an uncomfortable situation to be in. The best way to deal with this is with complete honesty and integrity. Approach the conversation with clarity of thought and set the tone for the conversation right at the start. State the facts, keeping the emotions out, and iron out the wrinkles. If it works it works, and if it doesn't, you will know you tried.

> *"What lies behind us and what lies before us are tiny matters compared to what lies within us."*
> **– Henry Stanley Haskins**

## Serena Williams

One woman who has used the strategies of calm, confidence, clarity, and communication is the famous tennis player Serena Williams.

As a young black girl from Compton, California, she didn't fit the mold of a traditional tennis player, but in spite of that, Serena Williams has gone on to become one of the most decorated female athletes in sports history. Success did not come easy for her, and she had to use the skills of 4Cs to navigate every step of her grueling sports journey with integrity and clarity. Her career has also been marked by persistent struggles on the tennis court and beyond.

From the very start of her career, Williams, alongside her sister Venus, encountered racial bias in what was considered to be a predominantly white and elite sport. She was contested by skeptics and was patronized by colleagues, the media, and sometimes the public, on the field and off.

She was either too timid or too strong, too weak or too aggressive. She was either too ambitious or too unfit. From being labeled as "unprofessional" to being criticized for her muscular build and strength, to being questioned about her actual capabilities, her treatment by media was often derogatory when compared with male players in similar situations. She was also often reprehanded for her apparently "non-feminine" physical features.

Ignoring all of these damned reviews and opinions about herself, she cultivated and nourished her sense of confidence and stayed calm in the face of the storms. She may have been aggressive on the field and in the heat of the moment, but she kept her communication and public interaction professional and limited. When she chose to speak up against the unfairness, she was labelled as emotional and irrational, and faced doubts and dismissals. But she won 23 Grand Slam titles, surpassing all other women in the open era, and yet struggled to find favour amongst the people for a very long time.

Instead of crumbling under severe bias and scrutiny, she chose to embrace her strengths and keep moving forward in her career. She had to prove herself at every stage of her career, and her fitness, agility, motivation, and mental fortitude were questioned repeatedly. Despite the unmatched achievements of 23 Grand slam titles and four Olympic medals, the failure at getting the 24th Grand Slam brought unfair criticism and questions about her legacy. While she was initially referenced as an example of why a woman should quit sports career after bearing a child, she eventually became a symbol of what working mothers can achieve.

Through her testing times and the demanding journey, Williams didn't just win titles – she changed the game. She opened doors for countless athletes of color and reshaped expectations for women in sports. She is a real-life example of why it is worthless constantly try to prove your worth. Instead, you should spend your energy doing what you need to do to get where you need to get – the rest is just noise.

*"Don't waste your energy trying to change opinions...do your thing, and don't care if they like it."*

**– Tina Fey**

## Taking Action:

1. **Identify your future self:** What would your future self look like. Imagine yourself ten to fifteen years down the road. Who are you as the successful, fulfilled person that you have become? Create your future persona who has achieved the goals, who has converted the dreams into reality. How does it feel to be that you? Make notes about how does the future you dress, talk, walk, show up? How does that future you think, feel and act? Slowly bring in those behaviours into the present time.

2. **Anchor in Your Calm Energy:** Calmness is the ground on which confidence is built. Pauses invoke trust and intrigue. Before any important meeting, event or decision, tap into your calm energy. Ground yourself with breathwork.

3. **Work on Your Confidence:** Pay attention to your physical, verbal, and vocal cues. Tap into the image of the future you, and draw inspiration from there. Imbibe the qualities, one at a time. Habits take time to change, repetition is the key to changing the habits.

4. **Dress to Kill:** Show up with confidence. Change your wardrobe if you need to – more structured clothing in neutral colours is known to have a professional impact, but wear what you can carry confidently

5. **Morning Meditation:** Breathe and chant *AUM*, with the A coming from the base of the navel, U coming from the chest, and M coming from the throat. Do this eleven times, then sit there in those vibrations and focus on your breath. Say to yourself, *"I am grounded, I am free. I am grateful. I am a channel to pursue the purpose of the Universe."*

6. **Practice Necessary Silence:** Avoid speaking too much, and choose silence over unnecessary words. Make sure you speak slowly and clearly. Practice using your voice at a calmer, slower pace, and with a lower pitch and a balanced tone.
7. **Avoid Filler Words:** Eliminate filler words like um, aah, just, because, etc.Do not hesitate to reframe your sentence, even if it is midway and you catch yourself going down the explanatory mode.
8. **Practice Clarity:** Do this with the following thoughts:

*"Our time and energy are finite – I must use them wisely."*

*"On days that I am more confident, I should go ahead and conquer the world. On the days when I have difficulty locating it, I must borrow it from outside."*

*"I don't have to prove my worth; it is evident for those who want to see it."*

*"People will look at me the way I look at myself. I must decide how good I want it to be."*

*"No one can make me feel inferior without your consent."*

*"Don't waste my energy trying to change opinions."*

*"It's not always about what we say, it is also about how we say it."*

RULE 5

# FOCUS ON YOUR PRIORITIES

*"Women belong in all places where decisions are being made."*

**– Ruth Bader Ginsburg**

When the doors are not opening for you, the challenges are different, but when you are trying to choose the door to enter, it is another big dilemma. Squandering away your time, energy, and money on things that are not your priorities is like living someone else's life hoping that someday you will live yours.

**If countries were led by women, there would be no war.**

Men and women are different biological beings, and these fundamental differences lead to the initiation of a neural pathway for information processing and decision making that is unique to their gender.

As we previously saw in Chapter 2, men primarily use the prefrontal cortex or the logical brain. They have a unique ability to keep the overreactive limbic system in the background. Nature does not function aimlessly – there is always a reason for the chaos that we believe the world to be in. Nature or Universe makes no decision randomly – there is a pattern in the chaos and there is a deeper, more complex connection between things beneath the surface, which we tend to ignore or may even be unaware of. Maybe it is a good thing for men to have a physical capability much larger than a woman's and to have a poor limbic system that is not always in fight or flight mode. While they gained a physical superiority over women – being more muscular and having more bone density and more physical strength – the lack of over impulsive reactionary behaviour prevents unnecessary harm to society. If and when such a lethal combination is present, the male body, with an overexcited limbic system, tends to drift towards psychotic, antisocial, or criminal behaviour. Imagine a room full of such men in the office meetings – women would need to run for safety.

> *"A woman is like a tea bag – you can't tell how strong she is until you put her in hot water."*
>
> **– Eleanor Roosevelt**

Women on the other hand, have superiority when it comes to mental and emotional fortitude. We may not be able to decide what we want to have for dinner while at a restaurant, but big family or business decisions are a breeze, partly because we are blessed with intuition. As per our observation in Chapter 2, each decision is based on carefully weighing in the logical and emotional, as well as experience-based data. The ethical department of the brain – the gut and the heart – are involved in all the choices we make, and rightly so. It is a well-rounded data analysis system that may suddenly decide to overthrow all facts and listen to the heart or gut for the final choice, plus sometimes the hormones hijack the entire process. And yet we do it, and do it well.

In addition to these biological differences, some extrinsic factors also play a role in how women think in business and leadership situations.

The social and family framework, the cultural expectations, the past experiences, the educational and experience-related disparity, as well as millennia of conditioning that women are not as capable as men – all of these and many more factors lead to differences between the thinking processes of men and women.

> *"The most common way people give up their power is by thinking they don't have any."*
> **– Alice Walker**

Women often focus on sustainable, long-term success, not just short-term wins, and they tend to do this while keeping in mind the importance of the relationship. They are better at risk mitigation strategies and team development – their balanced approach comes from having empathy and being a good listener, as well as having more nuanced communication skills, making them a right fit for sensitive issues. Their ability to manage complex interpersonal dynamics may be necessary to improve stakeholder alignment, although it takes a lot of confidence to achieve this. Sometimes women are better at de-escalating tensions and reaching mutually beneficial outcomes, and women often manage multiple priorities under pressure effectively, a skill many sharpen through their pursuit of a work-life balance. Their struggles and their place in society have given them an immense amount of resilience and adaptability in complex or chaotic environments.

* * *

How women blend professional and personal values, handle strategic boardroom conversations and build fulfilling careers is very diverse from the journey of a man. Something that plays a major role in our core strategic choices and the paths we traverse is the difference in the priorities between the two genders.

While men are mostly pretty good at separating work and personal lives, women look at life as a whole, and fulfillment at work is associated with fulfillment at home as well. It is a parallel universe for men, while for women it is a full circle of life.

**The parallel lives of men**

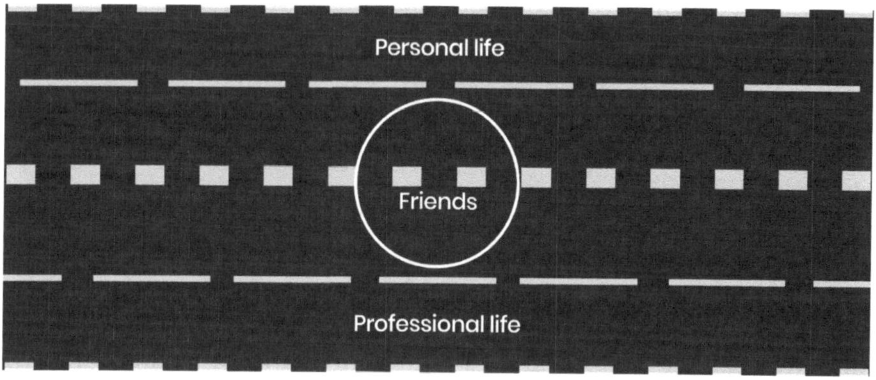


In their parallel universe, men want to excel and succeed at work, conquer the arguments, devise strategies for business growth, and build a reputation of power and success. In the parallel world, they want to be responsible husbands, fathers, friends, and providers of the best kind. For men these two universes run alongside each other but never intersect. There may be times when one path becomes wider and takes up some of the space from the other one, but they will eventually revert to their pre-determined forms. Everything in a man's life falls within the realms of either of these paths. Rarely both. Each of these paths go far and are well maintained, but they never merge – thereby success in one does not necessarily mean success on another. Similarly, failure or setbacks in one do not mean failure or setbacks in the other. Their unique ability to separate the two paths, usually protects them from their world collapsing all at once in times of chaos.

**The circle of life for women**

For women, the parallel paths do not serve a purpose in a wholesome life. We visualize our world as a whole, in the form of a sphere or a circle. The circle of life can have many priorities in one place together, all impacting different areas of our lives and the lives of others. Our work and career, our family and children, our friends and relationships, our spirituality and our beliefs, our goals and our values, our confidence and our strengths, our mission and purpose, our happiness and our hormones – all these fall into this circle and influence each other, as well as the entire state of the circle.

At the centre or the core are the most important things which tend to have the biggest influence, and as you move more towards the periphery, the things become less and less important and have trifling influence on the state of the circle. For all things that fall within this boundary, there is some attachment that holds it here. And as long as they stay, big or small, their power to influence the rest is undeniable.

Finding your priorities means finding out what your circle of life looks like. What are the priorities that you have within the realms of that circumference, that are responsible for bringing satisfaction to your every action? What does a fulfilled life mean to you? While there are some similar areas of significance that guide our decisions as women, there are others that are very specific and very unique to each one of us.

Balancing the many roles of businesswoman, professional, mother, and wife (and a lot more) – as much as these are deeply rewarding, they are also overwhelming. Identifying priorities in this complex landscape requires intentional reflection and strategic alignment. One of the most crucial parts of chasing our success or our fulfillment, is to be able to clearly identify our priorities.

There is no right or wrong, and there is no comparison – these priorities are unique to each one of us, and can be broadly categorized into areas that govern our experience in this lifetime, our personal growth, and how we contribute to this world.

There are many values that most of us women would agree to include in our circle- core values like integrity, freedom, success, love, health, growth, or faith. These values act as our compass and form the core of our circle. To identify what forms this core for you, start by identifying what matters most to *you* – not to society, not to your family, not to your husband/partner, not to your business or your peers. The best way to define this circle of priorities is to start at the core of it, which is purely you, then go more outwards, towards your immediate kin and what are the most important things that impact the core "you".

Once you have established their place in this core, the next step is to identify in your professional goals. What do growth, stability, innovation, legacy, etc. mean to you? What is the priority level of each these. Which concentric zone of the circle do these occupy today? What do you see changing in the coming years? Doing this allows you to mobilize your values and priorities, and modify them according to your life stage. Realize that priorities shift – some seasons you may focus more on business (e.g.,, a startup phase, early career opportunities, or a transition of career pathway), others on family (e.g.,, marriage, having children, looking after sick parents) – and that's okay. Expecting and preparing for these is important to keep the circle from falling apart.

As women, we also have a maternal instinct, which may or may not be evident today, but will become inevitable at some point of our lives. As a mother, what kind of presence do you want to be, or what kind of an upbringing do you want to give to your children? What are the values that you want to raise your children with?

Simultaneously, evaluate your personal relationships. What kind of partnership matters most to you – one with support, intimacy, shared responsibility? Who do you think you can share this life with, and are you willing to give it your all, even after nothing is left? No matter what stage of life or career you are in, personal relationships will always have a great impact on your circle of life, and that is an important reckoning. Even in the best of relationships there will be ups and downs, but how do you ensure open communication, and how far are you willing to go to keep the relationship intact will depend on what area of the circle it occupies today.

The core is fully ready to embolden you towards achieving your goals with clarity and purpose. Then you can start adding on the layers of the concentric circles. Look at your spiritual or energetic self, and try to identify the positives from the negatives. What drives you? What energizes you and what drains you? What else is there that deeply matters to you, that did not fall within the auspices of traditional questions? These questions will not only help identify the layers overlying the core of your circle, but they will also highlight any alignment (or misalignment) existing between your values and your actual life.

> *"The woman who doesn't require validation from anyone is the most feared individual on the planet."*
> **– Mohadesa Najumi**

The next layer of the circle is to identify the impact that you desire to create, the footprint that you plan on leaving. Learn to set boundaries and to determine what your "non-negotiables" are in each area of your life (e.g.,, date nights, one family meal every day, no work emails after 7:00 P.M., dedicated time with your spouse, weekly strategy time for business, etc.). Lastly, what are your support systems? While the internal support system of integrity, principle, values, motivation, and your dreams live within the deepest core of the circle, the external support system of family, friends, coaches, mentors, motivational gurus all conform themselves within the outer layers of the circle, indispensable but modifiable or adaptable.

Doing this exercise will help you understand how much of your resources – time and energy – are justified for each of those areas that fall in the circle. Some can be heavily draining on your resources, and the best way to approach these is to delegate, outsource, and to accept help, at home and at work. You don't have to do it all to have it all.

* * *

When men think about their lives, they might think about having a successful career with a good steady income so they can have their dream car, maybe their dream home, and to them, these are a given, these are their non-negotiables. They will do all they have to- in order for them to achieve these, since together they form their most basic idea of a good life and a good career. Beyond that, what their needs are or what their goals are will vary from person to person. What they need to be able to *reach* those goals will also vary, but their territorial nature justifies any action they need to take in order to maintain their dominance. It's a straightforward thinking process.

In their logical minds, it's not personal, nor is it unfair to destroy anything that remotely feels like a hurdle on their way to dominance. What this means is that if men perceive you as a threat in their career goal, they will go all out to destroy yours. It is more of that male mentality that is at play here than masochism. Right or wrong, they don't care if they think there is a threat to their livelihood and their dominance. If they feel that you are not a threat to them, however, they will likely do everything in their power to help you achieve your goals. You have to *ask* for help though, and understanding this concept is pivotal to navigating our paths to success as women.

There are times when we may come across other women who want to destroy our career or trample us under their shoes so they can get ahead, so we must identify those people in our lives and stay away from them as we embark on our journey of growth. Man or woman, when they have their territorial trait manifested, it is more of a devolutionary character, just as with animals.

* * *

Why do we need to prioritize? Why go through this exercise even though we may already know what we want? Because as successful women, we pursue more than just a good career.

We look at every area of life that falls within the circle, and we want to achieve balance and fulfillment in each of these areas. We pursue more than just work life balance – we seek integration and meaning across every domain of life. Fulfillment for us is not only about doing it all but also doing it perfectly, as well as living a life that feels authentic, purposeful, and aligned. While perfection is an elusive goal, it is OK to keep in our purse, but as an effort and not as an outcome. Because a perfect outcome is never something that is in our hands to control, while perfect effort *is*. Other than perfection, there are deeper elements at play when it comes to success and fulfillment, which is why we need to prioritize.

## Purpose-Driven Career

We like our careers to mean something beyond money or status. Our brains often seek to make a meaningful impact, to create profound value. We lead with a vision of leaving the world a better place for our children and the future generations. We take our ability to do something very seriously and often view that opportunity as a platform to lead change and transformation. We also want to make sure to be a good role model for our children to follow.

From that point of view, the purpose and the means with which we achieve that purpose are both equally important. We care about the influence our success has on other young women and we aspire to be a good and positive influence. We want to be able to open doors to opportunity to all women who come after us, and inspire our daughters to think big.

> *"Well-behaved women seldom make history."*
>
> **– Laurel Thatcher Ulrich**

## Positively-Aligned Relationships

While we invest completely in our career or our business, we always have the need for close emotional bonds with our spouse and our children in the background of our minds. We value intimacy, respect, and shared vision with a partner as the most important goals for our personal lives. While we are capable of being equally aggressive as men at work, and we may tap into that ability as and when the need arises, the foundation of our peace of mind lies in the crux of our personal relationships. A fulfilling marriage or partnership that provides us with mental stability, and a partner that nurtures the relationship with their understanding, motivation, and support is what we derive our energy from. Powered with that energy, we can fly with our dreams, while also staying grounded. We share deep, meaningful connections with our children and our friends. We seek positive mentors and strive to be a good mentor to others whom *we* can support. We hope to engage in nurturing relationships that energize us rather than drain us.

> *"The greatest happiness of life is the conviction that we are loved; loved for ourselves, or rather, loved inspite of ourselves."*
>
> **– Victor Hugo**

## Freedom and Autonomy

Given that our priorities are so diverse, one of the most important things for us is financial freedom and decision-making autonomy. After generations of suppression, women seeking these rights is a sign of great strength and courage in itself. Having our own business, or getting an education to enter the field of our choice, is one way of getting that freedom and autonomy to choose based on our needs, and to allocate our very limited resources of time and energy to only things and people that rejuvenate us or energize us. The ones who help us get one step closer to our goals, and instead of holding us further away from them. Financial freedom and the autonomy to make decisions make excellent food for our confidence, which in turn will power further actions that bring more financial independence and autonomy. It is a virtuous cycle that self-propagates. Creativity is another aspect of utilizing our freedom and energizing us.

> *"The question isn't who's going to let me, it's who's going to stop me?"*
>
> **– Ayn Rand**

## Personal Growth and Learning

One major step toward maturity is understanding that we are not competing with each other. We have our own journeys in this life – sometimes our paths may cross and we may travel some distance together – but these paths are separate. We may briefly meet on these journeys, or hold hands through tough times, but there is no need for us to feel obligated towards each other because we do not have the same goals. We may have the same career position we are vying for, but my goal with my life is not going to be the same as your goal about your own. The only competition we truly have is with who we were yesterday.

We prioritize growth from the point of view that we constantly compete with ourselves, and we seek out opportunities for self-improvement, whether through books, coaching, courses, or spiritual growth – this is the only way we can truly improve ourselves and get better at achieving our goals. Our hurdles and challenges are actually meant as lessons, and can be intentionally used for the purpose of personal growth. For women, success isn't just about goals – it's also about who we are becoming in the process, and whether we are able to identify this or not depends on the stage we are at on our journey.

> *"If you are always trying to be normal, you will never know how amazing you can be."*
>
> **– Amanda Fludd**

## Self-Care and Mental Wellness

Another reason that we should prioritize is our health and our wellness. Sometimes, in an attempt to do it all, we sacrifice sleep or personal wellness time, but we need to prioritize movement and physical activity while also working on our emotional resilience. Taking the time to participate in a personal wellbeing activity is too important to be neglected. We need to realize that if we don't do this, we will burn out.

I'm sure we are all guilty of doing this at some point. The guilt of not being there for our children all the time, or for not doing enough for our relationship weighs heavily on us because we do not understand that giving 100% of ourselves to our dreams does not mean that we are taking away from our relationships.

We need to give 100% of ourselves to everything that we are doing in the moment – 100% to our work when we are working, 100% to our children when we are with them, 100% to our spouse when we are with them, and 100% to ourselves when we have our "me-time." Having anything else on our mind does justice to no one and to nothing.

> *"I alone cannot change the world, but I can cast a stone across the waters to create many ripples."*
>
> **– Mother Teresa**

## Legacy and Contribution

As women, we also care about our legacy and our contribution. Have you sometimes thought about how you'll be remembered? If we are raising strong, independent children with good values? Are you a good mother? Are you building something that has an impact? Are you a good role model? Do you help in empowering other women? Identifying our priorities will help us give back through mentorship, philanthropy, or community involvement which is often a major source of meaningful work.

> *"I am not free while any woman is unfree, even when her shackles are very different from my own."*
>
> **– Audre Lorde**

## A Happy, Fulfilled Life

Identifying areas that bring you pure joy in your circle of priorities is very crucial to avoid burn out and allow you to enjoy life. When you are happy and joyful, you can bring joy to others and bring meaning to your work. Because at the end of the day, the only thing that matters is a meaningful life.

Travel and creativity are the biggest source of joy that we sometimes neglect. Joy can also be found in the small pleasures of life, like a morning of meditation, an afternoon coffee with a friend, a glass of wine with your husband, a game night with your children, or some personal wellness time. Fulfillment will elude you until you find joy.

> *"You have to act as if it were possible to radically transform the world. And you have to do it all the time."*
>
> **– Angela Davis**

Now that we have understood the reasons *why* it is so important to identify our priorities, it is time that we truly learn how to identify these priorities, because they may change. Life coach and founder of MindValley, Vishen Lakhiani's three most important questions we must ask ourselves are broad questions, and they will help identify all of your priorities regarding how you want to experience this life. You must identify your personal and professional goals, as well as identify what you need to do for personal or professional growth and how you see yourself contributing to this world.

I have done these charts to identifying the answers to Lakhiani's "three most important questions" for a few years, and have now refined them to create my own circle of life questions. I create this circle on paper for me at the end of each year, and it has now become a family activity, as my children and my husband and I do this together. This has helped us identify our own priorities, as well as understand each other's, and thereby help and support each other through the process. We make this into a fun activity during the last trip of the year, by the beach or on the mountains.

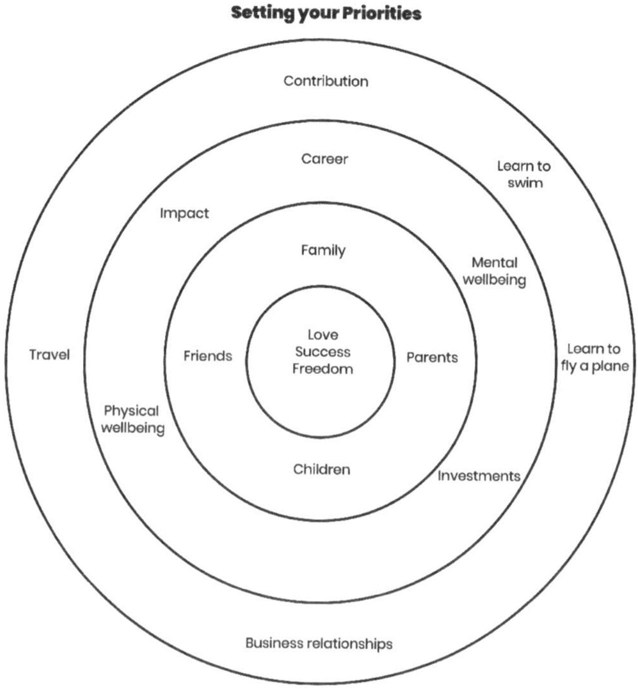


Through this bonding family activity, I achieve these goals:

- help everyone understand the importance of determining our priorities and what matters most to us, individually and as a family;
- reinforce the idea that we are one family and yet all have our own priorities and that we love and accept each others in spite of any differences in these priorities;
- help my children understand the fluid nature of priorities – that some will remain, some will grow, and some will dissolve;
- make a commitment to ourselves about our goals, and take small steps each year to move towards them, having accountability and ensuring that we keep each other on track;
- rid myself of some of the mother's guilt that we are all privy to. Declaring our priorities allows each one of us to positively allocate time to these, without guilt and without the fear of feeling neglected.

## Taking Action:

Here are some ideas from my circle of life, designed specifically for ambitious women balancing business, motherhood, and marriage. It will help you reflect and prioritize what truly matters to you. You may modify the questions as per your life situation, career, or areas of need.

### Part 1: Core Reflections

- What are my goals professionally?
- What does success and growth look like to me?
- What are my personal goals? How do I nurture my personal relationships with my husband, or with my children)
- What are my core values? (e.g., freedom, autonomy, love, integrity, impact)

### Part 2: Concentric Layers Reflection

- What are my non-negotiables? (e.g., honesty, resilience, positive energy)
- What creative or joyful activity do I want to engage in?
- What sport or physical activity do I want to engage in?
- What am I doing for my spiritual growth?
- What is one overambitious goal that I want to pursue? (eg. write a book, lead an investment fund)
- What are the activities that I need to undertake? (e.g., learning, networking)
- How am I going to contribute to the world?

## Part 3: Fulfillment Domains Checklist

- Am I energetically aligned with my goals? What changes do I need to make?
- Am I energetically aligned with my partner? What can I change to make our relationship better?
- What are the things that have been draining me this year? How do I eliminate these?
- What have I neglected, that I really need to focus on? (e.g., health, parents, friends)
- How did I grow/change/evolve last year?

RULE 6

# PLAY TO YOUR STRENGTHS

❝

*"New beginnings are often disguised as painful endings."*

**– Lao Tzu**

Success is never served on a plate; it is created on your feet.

It is never a good idea to wait on a charitable day to deliver what you need. There are only two ways to get something – to work for it or to ask for it. No amount of diversity or gender equality initiatives can bring to you your heart's desires, and even if it did, it is not going to bring you the satisfaction or the fulfillment you would receive by earning it.

Imagine asking for something that you don't deserve (yet) or you have not really earned – that would be called entitlement. The fruits of hard work are incredibly delicious, and are integral to building your confidence and taking you closer to a fulfilled life.

❝

*"Whenever you see darkness, there is extraordinary opportunity for the light to burn brighter."*

**– Bono**

There are times that you really work hard for something and are denied the results of perseverance. Asking for an opportunity and asking for what you deserve are very different from each other, and it is one of the crucial communication skills that women need every step of the way.

Due to hundreds of years of unfair conditioning, we lamentably live in a world that is substantially distorted in its views and perceptions. It is one thing to be *able* to accomplish a task or not, but it is a completely different thing to not even be given the opportunity to try.

Not surprisingly, opportunities differ significantly for men and for women in the workplace. Women tend to score higher in empathy, self-awareness, and social skills, which are necessary for conflict resolution, team building and team cohesion. Their long-term thinking capabilities, along with sustainable strategies to promote growth and mitigate risk, are stabilizing factors for innovation at the workplace. Women are also highly resilient and have a distinct ability to function well under stress or in chaotic situations.

While it has been observed that women bring a range of distinct strengths, advantages, and perspectives to leadership, the glass ceiling still fails them. In spite of these notable characteristics, they are still left behind when the doors of opportunities are opened. The societal and cultural norms are at play, but it is mainly the systemic organizational faults of the patriarchal work culture that have failed us.

*"Every wall is a door."*

**– Ralph Waldo Emerson**

Seeing men promoted to senior leadership roles while the women hit the "glass ceilings" is not an infrequent occurrence. The term "glass ceiling is a term coined in the mid 1980s as a powerful metaphor to describe the invisible systemic barriers that prevent individuals, mostly women, from advancing into leadership or executive positions, even when, or especially when, they are qualified for them. It would be prudent to say the "invisible hand" is that of patriarchy, and the concept of glass ceiling was given this name to put the blame on some invisible force.

These glass barriers see women being underrepresented in high-paying roles and overrepresented in low or mid-level positions. Men are more frequently assigned to high-stakes projects that lead to promotions, while women are often given execution roles instead of strategic leadership opportunities.

Another barrier to growth is the gender pay gap, which tends to favour men. Women are also frequently assumed to be less ambitious because they do not speak up for themselves, and the few who are assertive are labelled as aggressive. Men in the same situations are, of course, considered to be strong leaders.

> *"Everyone has something to contribute to this world. It's just a matter of being given that opportunity to do so."*
>
> **– Grace Hightower**

But most importantly of all, the difference is in how the men are evaluated on their potential and their assumed ability to do it all correctly, while women have to constantly prove themselves and are judged harshly for their decisions. Men are also advocated for by other men who could be mentors or seniors, and they receive powerful sponsorship from them. Heard of the "old boys club," anyone? Women on the other hand, find mentors, but lack the sponsorship to back their advancement.

*"Problems can become opportunities when the right people come together."*

**– Robert Redford**

No wonder women who face this turn to other options, including starting their own businesses or moving on to other places that value their skills more. Not that owning your own business is devoid of these barriers, but there is some consolation in the fact that it provides the autonomy to us to decide how we want to deal with our hindrances. Even in these circumstances, there are barriers to opportunities in other forms, like regulatory or legal issues, limited access to contracts, or the blocking of potential partnerships. Every business has its own risks and hurdles, and how we empower ourselves and make the best opportunity out of the situation at hand is the key.

*"Opportunities do not come with their values stamped upon them."*

**– Maltbie Davenport Babcock**

It is crucial to get out the victim mindset and instead focus on the opportunity that is hiding itself under the guise of a hurdle. The best opportunities are the ones that you create for yourself, and in order to do that, the first – and the most important – ingredient is resilience. The second is to play to your strengths.

*"Entrepreneurs are simply those who understand that there is little difference between obstacle and opportunity and are able to turn both to their advantage."*

**– Victor Kiam**

> *"A pessimist sees the difficulty in every opportunity; an optimist sees the opportunity in every difficulty."*
>
> **– Winston S. Churchill**

## Wu Zetian

Like most civilizations, China was, throughout much of its history, male dominated. For Wu Zetian to become the only female emperor in Chinese history and assume the role of the most powerful person in the country at the time, is a story of extraordinary ambition, resilience, intelligence, and strategy.

Wu was unusually well-educated for a girl of her time, learning to read, write, play music, ride horses, and study history and politics. For having been raised in a rigidly patriarchal society, she was assertive and intellectually sharp.

At a young age of 14, Wu entered the Imperial Court as one of the lower-ranked mistresses of Emperor Taizong, the second Tang emperor. While she was not favoured by the emperor as she did not bear any children for him, she used her position as an opportunity to observe and absorb the workings of Imperial politics and the bureaucratic workings of the court.

Upon Emperor Taizong's death, as was customary, all childless mistresses were sent to Buddhist convents to live as nuns. Wu was sent there as well, but her story was far from over. She found herself another opportunity to enter the Imperial Court, now as a mistress to the son of Taizong, Emperor Gaozong. This was controversial, but it was Empress Wang, the wife of the current Emperor Gaozong who brought her back into the court to divert her husband's attention from a certain consort named Xiao. Still young and beautiful, Wu had soon supplanted both

Consort Xiao and Empress Wang in Emperor Gaozong's affections. She eventually attained the rank of Empress Consort, giving her significant power and influence.

As Emperor Gaozong's health deteriorated, Wu began handling state affairs in his place and consolidating power. She was very tactfully building her own power base, promoting loyal officials while having others demoted, exiled or killed. Wu was soon effectively running the empire. Like many other men in her place would have done, she ruthlessly eliminated opponents, often using charm as well as fear as she saw fit. She established a strong bureaucracy and expanded access to government positions for people of lower birth, which was very unusual at the time. To garner more support for herself, she started promoting Buddhism, Buddhism being more open to female authority. In doing so, she was creating a space for herself as the female emperor before taking up the official title.

Wu gained the reputation of an able administrator, with a sharp wit and an extensive knowledge of history and literature. She also showed a remarkable ability to seek out and take out or weed out those who might someday pose to be a threat. When Emperor Gaozong died in 683 C.E., she was inarguably the most powerful person in China. In 690 C.E., she proclaimed herself the emperor, and founded the Zhou Dynasty.

As the emperor, she was responsible for bringing about major reforms in different areas like meritocracy. She promoted people based on skill and talents, thereby opening up the doors of opportunity for the less privileged and weakening the aristocracy in the process. She reformed the economic policies and reduced taxes, and supported public works like construction and impacting agricultural productivity. Her foreign policy was averse to wars, and with that aim, she maintained peaceful relationships with most surrounding states, instead maintaining control through a secret police and an intelligence network. She conducted military drills in Korea and central Asia to maintain the dominance in the region.

Most rulers in that age wrote history about themselves, and Wu commissioned Buddhist texts that portrayed her as the incarnation of Maitreya, the future Buddha, justifying her rule as divinely sanctioned. It not only established her persona in history, but also rid her of the need to find validation amongst the masses as a female emperor. She also had cultural interests, and encouraged poets and writers to create literary masterpieces. Artists, writers, scholars flourished under her reign.

As a leader, Wu was considered to be an able administrator and shrewd judge of character. She promoted and supported able men, and in return she received their firm loyalty. Her rule was benevolent to those who were no challenge to her, and ruthless to those who were. Even her enemies grudgingly praised her for her competence and decisiveness.

She is a one-of-a-kind figure in world history, not just Chinese history, who proved that leadership is not bound by gender, but by capacity, resilience, and vision. Her profound strategic outlook of balancing reform and repression to maintain power, her endurance and perseverance, and her literary talent and eloquent writing, are an acknowledgement to her powerful politics/reign.

As frequently observed, history does not judge strong female figures with much appreciation. While Confucian historians vilified her, modern scholars increasingly view her as a capable, visionary ruler who expanded the empire's power and strengthened governance.

Judgement of history is often harsh towards such decisive women who were able to seize the opportunity and grow to a position of power.

> *"When written in Chinese, the word 'crisis' is composed of two characters. One represents danger and the other represents opportunity."*
>
> **– John F. Kennedy**

## Giorgia Meloni

In October 2022, Giorgia Meloni became Italy's first female prime minister. Her journey to this position is a story of early political engagement, a steady ascent through political ranks, and the founding of her own party.

Her modest upbringing influenced her political outlook and commitment to national identity, and traditional values of hard work, family and national pride. At the age of 15, she joined the Youth Front, the youth wing of the Italian Social Movement (MSI). Either as a founder of the student organization called Gli Antenati (The Ancestor), or as a national leader of Student Action, she was actively engaged in educational reforms and soon she was elected as a councillor of the province of Rome. She led the student wing of the National Alliance sand then went on to become the first woman resident of the Youth Action (the youth wing of the National Alliance). This ascent from leading the Student Action to being the president of Youth Action was a journey of seizing the right opportunities at the right time, all the while fighting gender biases and ideological wars.

At the age of 31, her steadfast perseverance and the courage to speak up brought her the appointment as the minister of youth, making her the youngest minister in Italian history. She showed persistence and spoke up for the people she was representing, but most importantly, she aced the art of speaking up for *herself*, without which the political ascent would be a far-fetched dream.

When she hit the glass ceiling in her political career, Meloni co-founded the Brothers of Italy (Fratelli d'Italia) party, aiming to consolidate the right-wing political spectrum in Italy. She brought together the people with similar nationalist ideologies, and soon assumed the position of the party's president. Under her leadership, the party emphasized national sovereignty, traditional values, and a strong national identity, a cultural core that was lacking in Italy at the time. Her ardent pursuit of national interests and her fearless demeanour was the key to opening the door for her to the highest office in the country. In 2022, she became the first woman prime minister of Italy.

Her awareness of the pulse of the populace and her strong traditional values put her on a path to success. She sensed the frustration of the people with the liberal social policies, and seized the opportunity to position herself as a right wing, national pride-instilling leader that brought her party from oblivion to favour. Under her leadership, the government has focused on policies that internally strengthen the country and its citizens with national identity and traditional values, while also strengthening Italy's positions within the European Union and NATO with her pragmatic diplomacy.

*"Opportunities are like sunrises. If you wait too long, you miss them."*

**– William Arthur Ward**

Her remarkable journey from the margins of Italian politics to national leadership is marked by personal and political struggles, breaking through glass ceilings with courage, and perseverance and faith in her values. She often found herself as the only woman in the room where key political decisions were being made, and she faced years of political irrelevance before tuning into the pulse of the nation and boldly taking the opportunity to reform and reposition herself and her political party.

As a mother, she is often asked about the tension between political life and motherhood, a question rarely ever posed to a man in the same position. However, her ability to transform this critique into an opportunity to illustrate the ability of women to balance both, is a sign of prudence and strategic thinking.

> *"Our lives are defined by opportunities. Even the ones we miss."*
>
> **– F. Scott Fitzgerald**

### Listen to the Universe

It takes a lot of courage and resilience to stay on track towards your goals, especially when faced with monumental hurdles. It demands looking inwards and tapping into all you have, identifying your core strengths and adapting your methods to align them. The world may have conditioned us to be problem-minded pessimists, but it is important to evaluate our situation through an opportunity-minded lens.

If we only seek to destroy hurdles or relinquish them, that is an energy that is put towards a negative action. Instead, when we put on the opportunity-minded lens, our mindset will turn towards making the best use of the opportunity in a way that benefits us, an energy that is put towards positively recreating your circumstances. Any energy that is put towards a negative action is going to drain us and exhaust our limited resources. Any energy that is put towards a positive action and is founded in the mindset of gratitude and abundance, is going to bring an abundance of positive energy back. It may take some time for that to be evidently manifested in our lives, but know that it will.

> *"Victory comes from finding opportunities in problems."*
> **– Sun Tzu**

Sometimes all it takes is changing the way we look at our circumstances. Circumstances are ways to prepare us for the journey towards our goals, either through experience or through learning. They prepare us to take the risks that need to be taken to truly manifest our dreams.

The Universe has a unique way of presenting opportunities, and we just have to show our ability to listen. We often see an uncrossable hurdle and feel disheartened, but as we turn inwards, as we notice the functioning of the Universe, the layers of the hurdles peel off to reveal incredible opportunities for the willing.

In disguising the opportunity as a problem, the Universe is testing our desire, and our willingness to pursue our desire. We are being called to take the risk, to take the chance and convert it into an opportunity to reach our goals. To the courageous, it is a path, and to the others it is a deterrent. We either identify our opportunities and courageously tread our path, or we identify them and fail to tread the path out of fear. The Universe uses the challenges as a test to weed out those who are not deserving of it, or those who are not ready yet, while at the same time, these challenges are a way to empower us, and to strengthen us for what is to come. Resilience is one of those things that is a means as well as an outcome of the challenges we face.

Contrary to common perception, the Universe doesn't just give us one chance to identify our opportunities. The universal law of abundance applies to everything in nature and creation. The opportunities are presented to us again and again, just wearing a different robe every time. It is up to us to identify it and act upon it. By choosing to act upon it we perpetuate the cycle of resilience and success. On the other hand, by choosing *not* to act upon it, we let go of the opportunity, losing it altogether. Not because the Universe does not want to give it to us, but because we chose fear and convenience over courage to take the plunge.

This loss cannot be recovered and cannot be reverted. The Universe only takes something away from you when it perceives that you don't want it. Having the mindset of gratitude for any abundance is the key to keep it coming. Abundance says that there is enough and more for everyone; gratitude says, *"I am so grateful to deserve it and receive it and I pray for more."* Putting them both together is what attracts abundance in opportunities and in success.

> *"Not knowing when the dawn will come, I open every door."*
> **– Emily Dickinson**

There is a great amount of focus required to find the opportunities hidden inside of our challenges. If we don't see them immediately, it is usually just a matter of unfolding the creases and finding them hidden in those layers. Transformation of our hurdles into opportunities is about playing to our strengths, whether it is speaking up for yourself or taking decisive actions, nuanced communication skills and strategic self-advocacy are important in opening up the doors of opportunity. The notion that talking about our achievements without downplaying them is still unpalatable for women, and staying confident and visible even while being collaborative is a maze that we often get lost in. Tapping into our skills of assertive communication while using the power of silence helps in building influence and a supportive network.

The importance of finding sponsors, not just mentors, needs to be emphasized. While mentors provide guidance and support, sponsors open doors, and advocate for us behind closed ones.

Women's leadership networks are a good way to find mentors and to cultivate relationships with them so they can become our sponsors. Build a network of peers, mentors and role models, and contribute and learn from each other. Men are pretty good at this, and at asking for what they need, while women may get lost in translation when it comes to the ask. We are all guilty of this. Learning how to negotiate and be your own advocate when it comes to salary, job offers, roles or projects that may be risky, as these are perceived as a sign of ambition and are often gateways to ascending the ranks. Upskilling to improve business strategy, financial acumen, executive presence or other leadership or operational capabilities cannot be emphasized enough.

We can infer that women in business or corporate environments can cultivate the ability to seize opportunities by developing a combination of mindset, skills, and strategic actions. From self awareness and building confidence to changing our perspective towards challenges and opportunities, to developing hard and soft skills, these are all essential in forging ahead on our path to success.

It is important to distinguish when to persist and when to use personal setbacks (job loss, discrimination, failure) as motivation to start businesses, launch initiatives. It is not uncommon to see female entrepreneurs start businesses after career roadblocks or layoffs, turning "no" into "what next?"

*"Innovation is the ability to see change as an opportunity, not a threat."*

**– Steve Jobs**

It takes a lot of courage and a little bit of realization to face hurdles and identify them as innovative ways to solve problems overlooked in male-dominated industries. A stunning example of turning a setback into a stepping stone is Whitney Wolfe Herd, who left Tinder due to harassment issues. She created Bumble, an upside-down version of Tinder, a platform where women make the first move. Sometimes the best opportunities are ones you create or nurture over time.

> *"Turn your obstacles into opportunities and your problems into possibilities."*
>
> **– Roy T. Bennett**

Reframing failures as learning opportunities is a talent that men have in abundance. Borrowing this talent as women helps fuel our journey towards growth and success, and it is the key that opens many doors of opportunity. Eliminating the need for perfection allows us to say yes to opportunities that we may not feel ready for. Being open and ready to face challenges and learn along the way helps in building credibility.

> *"The true measure of success is how many times you can bounce back from failure."*
>
> **– Stephen Richards**

While we are thinking about how to open the doors to opportunity, it is important to realize that these doors to opportunity are many – they are plural, not singular. We can be so blinded by the challenges at hand that we only notice them a single one.

> *"When one door closes, another door opens; but we so often look so long and so regretfully upon the closed door, that we do not see the ones which open for us."*
>
> **– Alexander Graham Bell**

There are many paths towards our goals, and which one we choose is up to us. Notice them all, find them all, and then make a choice. Each path has hurdles and challenges, and each of these challenges will take us to the next level of the game.

*"Opportunities multiply as they are seized."*

**– Sun Tzu**

## Taking Action:

1. **Morning Meditation:** Focus on your breath. Inhale for five seconds, hold the breath for five seconds, exhale for five seconds, and then again hold the breath for five seconds. Repeat for seven to 10 minutes.
2. **Express Gratitude:** After the breathing, express your gratitude – for health, for wellness, for family, and for the opportunity to contribute to this world. Express gratitude for how the Universe helps you in achieving your goals and opening doors to opportunities.
3. **Focus on Cultivating the Mindset:** Be mindful of how you react to challenges and circumstances. Pause, check if you are being problem-minded or opportunity-minded, then change the perspective and seek the opportunities inside the challenges. If the answer is not immediately apparent, connect to the Universe to guide you. You can also ask for help from friends, your partner, or a coach.
4. **Find Your Network:** Join women's leadership groups, network, meet other successful women, and share the stories of struggles and of overcoming them.
5. **Discover a Mentor:** Find mentors and build good relationships. Next, ask for sponsorship. You can ask in this manner: "What would you want me to change or improve in, so that you can advocate for me for the role XYZ?" Sometimes it may be easier to start by asking for introductions or referrals.
6. **Seek Perfection in Effort, Not in the Result:** Do your best and expect the best, but be prepared for the worst and have a plan B.

RULE 7

# STAND YOUR GROUND

If you don't stand your ground, then the dreams that you built on it will crumble to pieces. It takes a lot of courage, patience, resilience, and integrity to strengthen the ground beneath your feet. While we are born with most of these characteristics, we discover and foster these through life's challenges, and others can be cultivated on the journeys we undertake. Sprinkled in between these core values are the skills that we develop along the way. It is the firm earth that supports, nurtures, and nourishes us, taking us through life's experiences. It is for us to walk, run, take flight and stay connected to our core values – this ground beneath our feet constitutes our character.

In many ways, standing your ground is more about what's deep inside than about what is outwardly visible. Much like an iceberg, you cannot judge the potential by what you see above the surface.

All the ancient scriptures explain the significance of character building. They define character as a melting pot of an individual's moral and ethical qualities that reflect their inner nature, as well as that which is reflected in their outward actions. They emphasize the concept of character as indicating a person's tendency to act in accordance with their values. Whether it is the Bible that is outlining the path to a virtuous life, or Gautama, the Buddha, who tells us to discover our world and give ourselves to it with all of our heart. The scriptures are teaching us, in their own way, that by confronting challenges that require us to tap into our strengths and our values, we open up the possibility of discovering what we are capable of, what matters most to us, and much like a sculptor painstakingly cutting and shaping a stone, thereby define and help build our character in the process.

*"It takes a great deal of bravery to stand up to our enemies, but just as much to stand up to our friends."*

**– Dumbledore**

The Bhagavad Gita is one such scripture where Lord Krishna teaches this whole process of character building to Arjuna, a prince and a warrior. Standing in the centre of the battlefield, about to wage a war with his next of kin and overcome with fear, shame and guilt, Arjuna is paralyzed by the fear of loss and willing to let go of the war.

Krishna then reminds him that a war of righteousness is his call to duty as a warrior, and forgoing this war is like giving up the duty and the responsibility. The Bhagavad Gita is about summoning all the strength and all the energies in order to do the duty, and yet remaining unattached to the consequences or the outcome. It is about focusing on righteous actions, and developing the patience and courage to accept what comes after. It is about taking the right action vs. choosing the safety net of *inaction*. It emphasizes that our potential and our purpose manifests not through cognition, but through action and through vital engagement with the world.

*"The world will not be destroyed by those who do evil, but by those who watch them without doing anything."*

**– Albert Einstein**

In life we are faced with challenges, some trivial enough to just affect our mood transiently, some monumental enough to shake us up and stumble us. But it is the strength of our character that holds us in place and doesn't let us fall and shatter.

Character, the ground beneath our feet, is the consolidation for what we carry inside of us, and what values and morals guide our actions and hold us steady on this earth, in this life. It is an ode to all the characteristics we have, as well as the lack thereof. Our character decides between what we think is right and what we think is wrong. And it is our character that guides how we respond to life's circumstances.

> *"Our lives begin to end the day we become silent about things that matter."*
>
> **– Dr Martin Luther King, Jr**

Character and confidence determine how much we cave in or buckle under pressure.

To "not give in" means to refuse to yield to either request, pressure, or temptation. It means refusing to succumb to someone else's demands or expectations. Staying strong and determined, even when faced with difficulties or resistance, is not an easy thing to do. It may even be safe to assume that it is more difficult than even starting the adventure towards pursuing your goals. One might think that knowing the opponent's intent is good enough to prevent giving in, but maintaining one's stance, resisting compromise, and not surrendering to external forces no matter how damaging it may seem to be in the short term, is the toughest challenge that will test each decision, each resolve, and each bold step towards our goals.

> *"Strong people stand up for themselves, but stronger people stand up for others."*
>
> **– Suzy Kassem**

It's fair to say that standing your ground and not letting others influence your decisions or actions is bolder than your decision to start in the first place. When you stand your ground on a belief, principle, decision, or a goal, staying steadfast in your beliefs – whether it involves you or others that you are responsible for – and not allowing external dominating factors to sway you, takes a lot of courage and conviction.

> *"In a world that demands you to obey the wrong rules: being rebellious is right."*
>
> **– Jenna Galbut**

### Margaret Thatcher

From 1979-1990, Margaret Thatcher was Britain's first female prime minister. During her long, polarizing tenure during the post-war, third Industrial Revolution, she earned herself the nickname of the "Iron lady," drawing comparisons with the original "Iron Lady," Golda Meir, the first female prime minister of Israel.

Margaret Thatcher was one of the most influential female political figures of the 20th century, in spite of having to undertake a major task of bringing the country out of the "Winter of Discontent."

She exemplified the art of persuasion and of not caving in to pressure. Not only she was able to devise policies that transformed the third

Industrial Revolution era in Britain, but she also showed an unflinching resolve when faced with pushback. She stood her ground and refused to yield to pressure. Her unwavering adherence to her values and principles and her ability to take tough decisions, and have the courage to stand up for them, is a testimony to her character and proof that the nickname "Iron lady" is well deserved.

> *"You must never be fearful about what you are doing when it is right."*
> **– Rosa Parks**

Prior to her holding the top office, she paved her way through extreme resistance from the old boys' club for being a woman in a man's space. From being ignored and unheard in party meetings to being labeled "overambitious" and "aggressive," her journey of speaking up was marked with assertive communication skills, a firm belief in her values and principles, and a single=minded focus on transforming post-war Britain.

There were times, on the envious tables full of male politicians, when she was considered to be unreliable because of her gender and was not considered suitable for leadership. Sometimes using her communication skills, sometimes the ability to stay silent, she continued to work towards her goals without compromising her values, and soon rising through the Conservative Party ranks to become Leader of the Opposition in 1975 – the first woman to lead a major British political party.

As the first female Prime Minster of Britain, Margaret Thatcher's timing in 1979 couldn't have been more challenging. After two Labour party's prime ministers' failed attempts at recovering the British economy, and a controversial decision by her predecessors to ask the IMF for an emergency loan, in return for billions of dollars of credits, Britain's public sector workers also went through monetary control through wage restrictions and were extremely discontent. A wave of strikes amongst the public sector workers, led to disruption of civil societal functions pre-empting the "Winter of Discontent."

To inherit such a Britain – plagued by high inflation, rising unemployment, and frequent strikes – could have been an insurmountable hurdle, especially as the first woman in office.

But not for her. Armed with an unflinching resolve, she embraced a fresh new economic approach of monetarism, ditching the then-favoured Keynesian approach. Despite sharp criticism, she stood her ground, firmly believing that controlling inflation was more important than the short-term outlook of unemployment figures.

While she was criticized for these decisions leading to only marginal improvements in the economy, the comparisons were more like a burden to prove herself rather than a fair evaluation of her capabilities with that of her male predecessors.

Her moment of recognition came during the unanticipated victory of Britain in the Falklands War in 1982 against Argentina. While she was urged to pursue diplomatic negotiation or withdrawal due to the islands' remote location and limited strategic value, Margaret Thatcher did not give into the pressure and instead sent the Navy to reclaim the islands. This military victory earned her the respect of the masses and led to a surge in the sentiment of national pride.

After a couple of years of smaller challenges, she faced a major miners' strike in 1984 when she inadvertently supported the decision to shut down mines. What had been lost, the ex-miners implied when the coal mines were shut down, was not so much a way of life as that whole confidence in what was real and what was fake.

Famous author George Orwell went down to live among the miners of Lancashire and Yorkshire for the book that became *The Road to Wigan Pier.* His book documented all the ingrained ironies of that quest: "In a way it is even humiliating to watch coal miners working," he wrote. "It raises in you a momentary doubt about your own status as an 'intellectual' and a superior person generally. It is brought home to you, at least while you are watching, and that it is only because miners sweat their guts out so that superior persons can remain superior."

When their frustration turned into a miners' strike, Margaret held her position and stood firmly on her decision, despite being accused of destroying working-class communities and escalating conflict. She refused to negotiate or back down, asserting that the strike was an attempt to bring down her government, and that her decisions that led to shut down uneconomic mines was right for the country. She built up coal stockpiles in advance, and passed laws to reduce union power as a way to prepare for the pushback. The strike collapsed, weakening union power for decades and solidifying her reputation as a tough, unyielding Iron Lady.

She also brought radical reforms and privatization to other state-owned industries like air transportation, telecommunications, and oil and gas, thereby curbing the power of unions, cutting public spending, and deregulating markets. She was met with a tremendous amount of backlash and accusations about being a capitalist. Not to be perceived as fragile, she stood her ground yet again, insisting her belief that individual responsibility and free enterprise, free from government control and free from union pressure, were keys to national benefit.

Empowered by this victory, she introduced a highly unpopular flat-rate community charge (poll tax) that was again met with extreme public outrage and riots. While her own party warned her to back down, she refused to back down or even reverse the policy. This was her downfall, the one that led to her departure from the role of prime minister. Even in that moment of resignation, she acknowledged her firm belief and conviction that her policies were all in national interest. She chose to step down after a turbulent 11 years and resign, instead of giving in to the noise around her.

> *"Most of the important things in the world have been accomplished by people who have kept on trying when there seemed to be no hope at all."*
>
> **– Dale Carnegie**

The Iron Lady nickname was accorded to her by Russia during the era of Cold War. She stood strongly against Communism, aligning herself with her allies. During this key partnership with the likes of Ronald Reagan, she maintained independent judgment in national interest. She personified the uncompromising, intellectual, confident women who only knew how to do her job and did not care about being liked for doing it the way she thought was right. She showed how we could be stubborn when it comes to our values, principles, and vision, and not give in to pressure from dominating forces.

> *"Great spirits have always encountered violent opposition from mediocre minds."*
>
> **– Albert Einstein**

Stand for what is right, even if it means standing alone. It is our character that gives us the ability to do what needs to be done, and cultivating a good solid character is consequential in giving us the inner strength to follow through with our resolve, while also giving us the reputation of someone who has the guts to pursue their dreams, no matter how difficult the path.

"

*"What's the point of having a voice if you're gonna be silent in those moments you shouldn't be?"*

**– Angie Thomas**

## Develop character as a way to stand your ground

We're born with some qualities that make up our character, and some we learn through our upbringing. But there are some aspects of our character that develop as we go through life and have experiences, and it's within our power to strengthen our character with the choices that we make.

First and foremost, we need to identify our core values. This is the part that we are born with and learn through our upbringing. Sometimes these values are cultivated along the way as a result of what life throws at us.

There is profound value in identifying our moral compass. The values that we feel the strongest about, or the words that define us the most, are our core values. These are non-negotiable values that are underlying every decision we make and everything we stand up for. These are some things that will always be on our minds, behind everything we think that is right or wrong, and everything that we do and experience. These constitute the ground beneath our feet – firm, unshakeable and nurturing.

"

*"Courage isn't having the strength to go on – it is going on when you don't have strength."*

**– Napoleon Bonaparte**

We need to then try to identify what it means to us to stand our ground. While identifying our values is just one thing, the composition of our character is mainly about our decision to really stay true to our core values, even in times of adversity. What are the things you will not compromise on, no matter what anyone else has to say to you? What are the values that you will truly not abandon, no matter what the circumstances are?

Thinking of worst-case scenarios, as well as best case scenarios, is necessary to really bring ourselves face-to-face with our true core values. If honesty is one of yours, but from time to time you resort to lies to avoid the inconvenience of standing up for it, then it is not your core value. Identifying core values is about being brutally honest with ourselves – nothing can be your core value if you don't resonate with it every single moment of your life, regardless of your circumstances. For physicians, for example, one of the most important core values is honesty and integrity. These may be intrinsic or cultivated, but they need to be present. No matter what happens, compromising on those is not an option, as patients' health and lives are at stake.

There are times when our heart tells us to stand up for what we think is right. But how do we stand our ground? All of us are different, and the situations in which we find ourselves can be way more complicated than what they appear to be. Standing our ground can look like many things and we may use one or more of the following methods to do so.

## Be calm, composed and decisive

Sometimes wavering on our decisions is justified in our minds because we do not want to take a stand. It is easier to *not* make a decision, because we have it in us to stand by our decision and not cave in to pressure. Do we feel prepared for the outcome if it is adverse? Do we feel confident that the decision is truly the best one for the current situation? Being calm and composed, evaluating the risks and benefits, and being prepared for the outcome is the least we need to do.

## Know when to say "no" and when to not be agreeable

There is a substantial difference between being nice and not speaking up because we're afraid or unsure. As women, being agreeable comes as a natural trait, and sometimes it may be perceived as a sign of weakness. Psychiatrist Dr Jordan Peterson says that the more agreeable we are, the worse we are at negotiation or conflict resolution in our favour. Similarly, not being able to say "no" is another sign of high agreeableness, and thereby a weaker ability to stand your ground.

> *"Your silence gives consent."*
> **– Plato**

## Work on building your resilience and patience

Resilience contributes to building good character like nothing else, and resilience comes from how we deal with difficult situations or difficult people. Growth lies beyond the comfort zones, and it takes patience, courage and resilience to get out of the comfort zone.

It's a given that not caving in and standing your ground is an act of resilience and patience. How many times as women have we taken bold steps or brave decisions, only to get pushback from others? Sometimes this resistance comes from men in the field, other times it is an act of envious women, who cannot be as bold. But these experiences come to us to strengthen our resilience and our character, so weather the storm with patience and courage.

## Persevere through challenges

Tough times don't last, but they do test your resolve. Tough people don't persist, but they test your character. These challenges are just a chapter in your life, so don't make it your whole story. Observe, stand your ground, build character and move on. If you have the right facts in place, and if you have faith that what you decided is the right thing to do, it is easier to not give in to pushback, criticism, and pressure from dominating forces.

Character shows in the actions that you take, as well as the actions that you do not take. For example, when you're working as a team, if you defend the action of your team in the face of a bad outcome, because you know the team is doing the right thing and taking the right actions, that aligns with your character. Similarly, turning down a partnership because the prospective business partner uses unethical practices to increase revenue is an action not taken to remain aligned with your character.

## Identify the dominating forces that are jeopardizing your decisions

If there is obvious direct obstruction on your journey towards your goals, or an open conflict, it is easier to identify, and therefore, easier to handle. What's more complex are situations like passive aggression, backhanded aggression, or something like being stabbed in the back. These people are driven by envy and insecurity, not because of where you are in your life, but because of where you are in relation to where *they* are. To preserve your sanctity, these situations need to either be ignored or hand, or handled very delicately.

## Work with people, not against them

Assertive communication and letting go of the need to be liked by all are crucial to standing your ground. Being polite yet firm, thoughtful yet non-agreeable, kind yet assertive, and not letting emotions get in the way of the conversation gives an impression of a strong confident woman. Maintaining mutual respect, even in times of disagreement, is a sign of good character. When it comes to narcissists or passive aggressive or high-conflict individuals, these communication rules may fall flat. Their insecurities, fears, and unresolved anger prevent a mutually respectful communication. The best way to handle such situations is to eliminate your emotions, minimize your words, and rely heavily on the power of silence.

> *"Raise your words, not your voice. It is rain that grows flowers, not thunder."*
>
> **– Rumi**

Know that there are things that are completely out of your control. What do you do when they are not physically present in front of you, but are orchestrating your destruction behind closed doors? The best ammo that you have for this is : "Keep calm and carry on." You don't have to give them any energy at all; being cordial and keeping the conversation to a minimum is key to not empower them with unnecessary oversharing or unintentionally show your emotions. Slowly but steadily, move on from the hold they have on you.

> *"Courage is what it takes to stand up and speak; courage is also what it takes to sit down and listen."*
>
> **– Winston Churchill**

It is essential to stand your ground, because no one else will do it for you. There are those who would give anything to see you fall, but you must never give them the satisfaction of doing so – instead, hold your head up high, put a smile on your face, and stand your ground. The best revenge you can give is to become so secure in your character that the negativity no longer bothers you.

Being able to admit when you're wrong is important, but so is standing up for yourself when you are right. In the world that we live in today, and the women that we are, it is extremely relevant not only to be able to speak up for ourselves but also that we summon all our courage and character to speak up for those who can't speak for themselves. Stand your ground even when nothing of your own is at stake. Be a physician that speaks up against the vaccines that are not tested, or report research that is incorrectly conducted. Be a journalist that cares for real news, and speak up against propaganda that is being used against public interest. Be an engineer that speaks up against the unethical use of technology that could harm unassuming users, especially children. Be a leader that stands up against the bureaucracy and political persecution of honest, law-abiding citizens.

## Use your voice

What's the point of having a voice if you're going be silent in those moments you shouldn't be?

In Chapter 5, we discussed the circle of priorities, and responsible action may be one of those for you. If that is the case, then the absence of responsible action is going to mess with the peace of your mind, and thereby impact everything in our circle. We may choose not to take a call for action, but only so long as our character and peace of mind permits us.

If history is recorded honestly tomorrow, it will elucidate that profits bend moral boundaries, and as a woman, one thing that weighs heavy on our shoulders is to do right unto all for the generations to come.

Dr Cassie Means speaks up in the interest of public health, standing up against the pharma industry and the food industry controlling the overall health of the people, by interfering with the decision-making process of regulatory bodies like the FDA and the CDC. She puts her time and resources into educating people and the authorities to bring about a change.

Similarly, Frances Haugen, a former Facebook employee, exposed the dark mechanics of social media and teens' mental health. Her actions led to renewed calls for tech regulation and algorithm transparency.

Riley Gaines, an American swimmer raises her voice to protect the sanctity of women's sports from transgender athletes who, accept it or deny it, have male genes, male hormones, male muscles and male bones.

And we cannot miss the brave Australian female founder of Giggle for Girls, Sal Grover, an app that was created as a safe space for women and girls to engage and connect. The app was accessed by a transgender "woman" named Roxanne Tickle, who is a male by birth, genetics, and biology. When the woke Western courts unlawfully ruled against Sal and penalized her, she did not back out – not just for herself, but also for the hundreds of thousands of women on her platform.

Sal, with the help of her female lawyer Bridie Nolan put up a brave front and stood her ground, highlighting the fact that women are now not just fighting against men for their rights, but a few other gender dysphoric people as well, individuals who want to invade women's physical and virtual spaces.

These are just a couple of examples of women who risked everything to expose corruption, injustice, or hidden truths, often facing personal and professional retaliation and yet holding their ground for a greater cause.

*"Believe in yourself and all that you are. Know that there is something inside you that is greater than any obstacle."*

**– Christian D. Larson**

## Taking Action:

1. **Meditate:** Do the AUM chant 21 times (again, A from the base of the stomach, U from the chest and M from the throat) every day as a source of strength and courage from the Universe. While building your character or standing your ground is not as much of an action as much it is a way of life, on days when you are not sure, you can follow these steps to tap into your inner strength.
2. **Identify Your Core Values:** Name your non-negotiables, and do not look for validation.
3. **Stay Calm:** Be composed and decisive, and be prepared to be challenged on these and to stand your ground.
4. **Learn to Say "No":** Practice assertive communication. When faced with high conflict people, start first with silence, and then ask for intent behind their words. Ask directly if the words were meant to be helpful or hurtful. Sometimes a simple, "Thank you, but I am not looking for advice at this time," is effective; sometimes just staring in their face and saying, "Say that again" or "Hopefully that gives you some peace" and walking away works too.
5. **Build Strength:** Work on building your resilience, patience, and communication skills, as well as the art of staying silent. Practice, practice, practice. Know that after the first two to three times, it gets very easy.
6. **Name the Hurdles:** Identify the dominating forces that may interrupt your journeys, and be prepared to handle them with dignity, resilience and the art of non-agreeableness. Learning when

to speak, minimizing your words, and using more of your silence in these situations is not easy, but keep practicing.

7. **Take a Stand:** Stand up for yourself and for others who cannot stand up for themselves.

RULE 8

# LET GO OF NEGATIVE FEELINGS

Society approves and praises women who sacrifice their ambition, but no one knows, or pays attention to how incomplete that woman feels inside of her.

As women, we are burdened by the haves as well as the have nots. When we don't have the career that we desire, we feel unfulfilled, and yet when we have it, or are on our way to it, our happiness is clouded by the many negative feelings that arise along the way. The primary cause of this is our striving to achieve perfection in every role that we play in our lives. These negative feelings not only prevent us from seeing our past achievements in good light, but they also obscure our vision of the future.

It is a well-acknowledged fact that women have to jump through insurmountable hurdles to make it to the top of their industry or of the corporate ladder, and even when they're outperforming their coworkers, women still bear the brunt of criticism – professional as well as personal.

A woman in business is way more than just a woman. She is a leader and a spiritual being focusing on meditation, fitness, and self-improvement. She wakes up early, donning the robes of a mother or a wife prepping breakfast and lunch for school. Then she heads to work and transforms into a boss babe, perhaps carrying the responsibility of the manufacturing unit, or of the financial department, sometimes playing

CEO, CFO, a marketing lead, a head of operations. Sometimes she dons other hats, and most of the time she is donning more than one.

During a typical workday, she juggles work with her personal calendar, her children's school and extracurricular calendar, the meetings for another passion project, mentoring interns or other young students, scheduling and attending to healthcare appointments for parents or in-laws, and finding some "me time" to work out, go for a massage, cook a meal, or plan the next holiday. Sometimes there may be added duties, depending on the stage of the business or age of the children, but at all times, there is one more responsibility hanging over her head: to do it all right, to be perfect.

We will come back to this primary source and the theory of Aligned Perfection – first lets understand and eliminate the secondary causes of pain and disarray. It's important to know that every single one of these challenges is connected to the mindset.

As a woman business owner or a corporate leader, the flaws in our mindset will show up in the form of a wide range of negative emotions that are caused by the unique pressures, expectations, internal, and barriers we face.

## Guilt

While the most common negative emotion that men experience during their careers is stress, the most common negative emotion for a woman is guilt. Guilt can come from being absent from your family or children when they need you or from feeling that you are not present enough at the workplace, even if it is only to socialize and mingle with your colleagues. "Mother's guilt" is an intense emotion for working mothers, partly driven by societal norms about maternal presence, and partly driven by the feeling of not being a perfect mother. These feelings of guilt are truly never ending, no matter the stage of the career, no matter the age of the children, and no matter how far we have come. No success can sweeten the bitterness of mother's guilt.

On one hand, the guilt consumes our satisfaction about our personal lives because of our perception that we are failing our children, partner or the family due to work demands. On the other hand, needing flexibility at work or time off for emergencies or other daily matters, the guilt at work dilutes our job satisfaction. The emotional burden of the feeling of depriving those who need us a is the biggest burden faced by most career-oriented women.

> *"Obstacles don't have to stop you. If you run into a wall, don't turn around and give up. Figure out how to climb it, go through it, or work around it."*
>
> **– Michael Jordan**

## Impostor Syndrome and Self-Doubt

Persistent self-doubt, even in the face of accomplishments, is a trait that is not specific to, but more deeply rooted in, women. Excessive self- doubt clouds our ability to objectively and realistically assess our competence and skills, even despite obvious achievements. This is amplified in male-dominated environments, where women are usually judged and scrutinized very harshly and are required to prove themselves over and over again.

How many times have you been asked about your achievements, and then you responded by attributing it to external factors or to good luck or good timing, or just negating the praise, by saying, "Oh it's not much really, in front of what *you* have done." This is a sign of imposter syndrome, and it is important to know that it affects early-stage entrepreneurs, as well as highly accomplished women at the peak of their success – even the most admired women in the field of acting or modelling fall prey to this.

> *"If you hear a voice within you say you cannot paint, then by all means paint and that voice will be silenced."*
> **– Vincent Van Gogh**

## Burnout and Exhaustion

The weight of the dominating emotions of guilt and self doubt, along with the difference in expectations for men and women at work, is substantial. Many studies have shown the difference between men and women at the workplace, with studies by McKinsey and others in this field showing that women need to work way harder and way longer to prove that they are worth the raise, promotion, or position. Women feel constant pressure to work extra hard to show that they are deserving of the role.

The external pressure, created by societal norms, adds to the internal pressure of guilt. Thereby the intense pressure to juggle high-stakes decisions and put in long hours, paired with guilt and emotional labor, is what eventually leads to chronic fatigue and mental burnout. Lack of adequate support at work and at home exacerbates this feeling of fatigue and exhaustion. The reality of burnout is also that every high-performance, high achieving, ambitious woman thinks that they can never burn out. But, one fine day, either the physical or the mental signs of exhaustion and burnout will show up, and the more we ignore these signs, the more they will increase in intensity.

> *"Burnout is what happens when you avoid being human for too long."*
> **– Michael Gungor**

## Isolation

Women in business, or in other decision-making positions, usually find themselves feeling alone or being misunderstood. They are judged for their tough decisions, or their assertive communications, and deemed authoritative. There is no company that they find in their unique challenges. They often find themselves being judged left, right, and centre- from being too emotional to being insensitive, from being weak and unreliable to being rude, authoritative or too bossy . There are few peers around them who share their identity or experience, partly because there aren't many women in their roles and positions, and partly because the women peers that are *in* those positions do not always network together and barely find time to support each other.

> *"Success is a lonely road. It is an isolation chamber where your deepest fears and ambitions co-exist."*
>
> **– Robert Greene**

## Frustration

What gender bias, unequal pay, or the glass ceilings do, is add to the frustration of hard-working, high-performance, and high-achieving women. Women find themselves in positions and situations where upfront or very inconspicuously, they are being expected to do more emotional or organizational labor at home or work, and in spite of putting in all of those extra efforts, about 76% of top-performing working women receive negative feedback from their bosses, compared to just 2% of high-achieving men.

The study, which analyzed performance reviews for more than 23,000 workers across over 250 organizations, concluded that "Men mostly receive feedback about their work: they're developmental observations, they're constructive. While for women, the positive observations are not generally about the work – they're about the woman's demeanor, personality, or disposition. We tend to relate to women in the workplace based on how they make the people around them feel, rather than the work that they're doing."

So the evaluation of a man is purely work-related, or related to his ability to make professional connections and speak, while for a woman it drifts more towards social skills – and more precisely, the social skills that others perceive that she carries or lacks – in place of the quality of the work that she's doing. This builds up, and adds to feelings of frustration, anger and dissatisfaction.

> *"You don't need to doubt yourself – plenty of people will do that for free!"*
>
> **– Francis Shenstone**

## Resentment and Discouragement

The expectation of personal and professional excellence, along with the burden to carry disproportionate responsibilities, and every single time, hitting into the barriers of the walls of the old boys' club, or the glass ceilings, leads to frustration, and eventually, resentment. Resentment toward partners, coworkers, or systems that expect women to carry disproportionate responsibilities. And the perception that even after all the hard work and all the years of sacrifice, the future of a woman's career depends on the man at the top. After many years of this, he resentment and the discouragement are hard to not let brew.

> *"Don't aim to break the glass ceiling, aim to shatter it!"*
>
> **– Matshona Dhliwayo**

## Anxiety and Dejection

The constant flow of judgement – from well-wishers and not-so-well-wishers – is tough to strike away. Even if we can do so momentarily and move on with our work, the seeds are still sown about the fear of failure, anxiety, or unnecessary comparisons to our peers, and the pressure to be perfect in every role we play as women is turned on. This leads to moments of anxiety, dejection, thoughts of failure and incompetence. Eventually, after repeated cycles of this, we experience anxiety, stress, and difficulty in coping.

> *"One of the greatest discoveries man makes, one of the great surprises, is to find he can do what he was afraid he couldn't do."*
>
> **– Henry Ford**

## Shame

The profoundly impactful feeling that women usually do not acknowledge is the feeling of shame. Men and women are both prone to shame, but the triggering factors for each are gender specific. Men experience shame if they are perceived to be too weak to care for and protect those for whom they are responsible, or at their inadequacy at being the provider. Women, on the other hand, have many triggering factors of shame, ranging from feelings of inadequacy or imperfection to feelings of not meeting expectations, to being made to feel overly ambitious. Some factors are even related to physical appearance or aging.

At times, guilt and shame are considered to be the same, but there is a big difference – while the former focuses on our actions or what we do, the latter is more deeply connected to our being, or who we are. They are the two ends of the spectrum, where the objectivity goes down as we move from guilt to shame. While guilt says, "I did this wrong, or "I made a mistake," shame says, "I am irresponsible," and "I am not good enough."

> *"Nothing silences us more effectively than shame"*
> **– Dr Brene Brown**

## Anger and Regret

At the helm of all of the scrutiny, internal and external, and all of the discrimination – hitting the glass ceilings, facing unfair judgements and microaggressions, being talked over or undermined – is the frustration, which, over the years, builds into anger.

The feeling of not being in control of our own lives, in spite of giving it our all, leads us to feelings of anger or regret. And because of our life is one big circle, instead of the parallel lives of men, regret is also exaggerated by other areas of our personal lives – not being present for our families or children, missing milestones, or not being able to pursue personal goals. All of these feelings of regret, mixed with the frustration at work, lead to the build up of anger and dissatisfaction with ourselves or our circumstances.

> *"You wouldn't worry so much about what others think of you if you realized how seldom they do."*
> **– Eleanor Roosevelt**

## Fear

As we try to do it all, and have it all, sometimes not having control of the outcome, and relying on others' perception of us to prove our worth, leads to fear of failure. Even as we learn to make tough decisions and stand our ground, there is always the fear of being misunderstood as too aggressive or too ambitious. The constant juggling of personal and professional lives, and internal and external factors impacting these, creates the fear of losing it all, which is founded on the principle that sometimes extremely capable or successful women are perceived as a threat by insecure, competitive men who seek to destroy them.

> *"There is only one thing that makes a dream impossible to achieve: the fear of failure."*
>
> **– Paulo Coelho**

## Pressure to Be a Role Model

Feeling burdened by the expectation to be the perfect woman, perfect boss, perfect mother, and to be a perfect role model for your children, as well as for other women around you, is a pressure that we put on ourselves. We take it upon ourselves to stand up for and to represent all women, particularly when it comes to underrepresented industries or leadership spaces mainly dominated by men.

The reality of the emotional landscape that women experience is complex, and the complexity increases for those in leadership roles or high up the executive ranks. And while we may have looked at these emotions individually, there is usually a mesh of several of these that we are each facing at the same time. Dealing with these negative emotions is not easy, and while I wish this would be like a game of pool, where we use one stick to push one white ball, to hit all the negative emotions, slowly, strategically, at our own pace, in reality these work more like a game of tennis, where you have to hit the ball as it comes to you, at a fast pace, and have to run around constantly, making sure you are hitting the ball hard out of your side of the net.

> *"Don't wait. The time will never be just right."*
> **– Napoleon Hill**

## Helen Keller

Helen Keller, known for her extraordinary achievements as a deaf and blind person, endured deep emotional and psychological struggles – and yet she did not let her disability come in the way of experiencing life fully. She constantly strived for improvement, and refused to be limited by society's expectations. It was common perception at the time that someone who was both deaf and blind could never be educated, but Helen, with the help of her teacher Anne Sullivan, defied the limits of her disabilities and proved otherwise. Her journey to becoming an author, activist, and symbol of resilience was marked by many internal and external hurdles.

In early childhood, due to the inability to communicate, she experienced extreme rage and frustration. These sensory impairments made her feel completely cut off from the world and imprisoned within herself, and she experienced extreme isolation and loneliness.

She overcame the despair and hopelessness with the curiosity to learn and a desire to find her strengths. Not only did she learn to read, write, and speak, but she also mastered multiple languages like French, German, and Latin. She defied educational norms and graduated from Radcliffe College in 1904, becoming the first deaf-blind person to earn a bachelor's degree.

Her life was never completely free of fear, confusion, or grief over the missed experiences of her life, and in those moments of despair, she doubted her ability to contribute meaningfully to the world, leading to more negative feelings of self-doubt and insecurity. She questioned her own capacity for academic success and feared judgment from others.

It is important to highlight here that while language empowers you to learn, understand, wonder, and express, it is the same ability to think, learn, and understand that also makes you feel the negative feelings of self-doubt and insecurity. This is why children rarely face these at a young age, and only develop these feelings as we condition them to the ways of the world. Helen found a great mentor in Anne, who channeled her emotions in the right direction and ensured that the conditioning was more empowering for her than otherwise.

*"Alone we can do so little; together we can do so much."*
**– Helen Keller**

As she put herself out there, her courage and determination earned her other mentors like Alexander Graham Bell and Mark Twain, who encouraged her to speak and write publicly. She channeled her energies towards activism and advocacy, in support of disability rights, women's rights, socialism, and racial equality, giving herself a sense of mission and direction. This was only possible for her after deep spiritual searching allowed her to accept her physical disability as just that, and not something that could limit her spirit. She created Braille to empower the blind and deaf and open their doors to the world of possibilities, and during her times of inner turmoil that crept up every now and then, she found peace in music, poetry and nature

She co-founded the American Civil Liberties Union (ACLU) and worked with the American Foundation for the Blind for decades. As she forged her path from disability to enablement, she faced harsh criticism for her opinions and her activism. While people acknowledged her courage in overcoming her disabilities, they expected her to stay in her box. But despite the pushback, she lobbied for equal access, rehabilitation, and employment for the blind and deaf. In a time when disabled people were often institutionalized or hidden away, she stood in the limelight and demanded they be treated with dignity and inclusion. She lobbied for women's rights calling out that women were being deliberately held back in society and deserved full representation politically and elsewhere.

Helen symbolises the ability to be fully oneself. She refused to be just a symbol of inspiration, and was bold, opinionated, and unafraid to challenge public expectations. She insisted people see her as a whole person – not just a "miracle story," but also as a woman with ideas, convictions, and the strength to stand behind them. She was a trailblazer who overcame personal disabilities, and also spoke up against external demons for justice, equity, and human dignity.

## Cindy Crawford

Decades after Helen Keller, not much has changed. Ambitious and daring women face these challenges worldwide. Iconic supermodel Cindy Crawford has faced significant personal struggles, unfair treatment, and low emotions. Behind her commanding runway presence and glamorous public image is a story of navigating dark paths, as well as one of overcoming barriers through self-reinvention and quiet fortitude.

Grieving the loss of her brother to cancer, Cindy channeled pain into purpose by getting involved in cancer-related charities, keeping her grounded in an industry engulfed by fame and grandeur. Being an outsider, she did not "fit" in the modelling industry of the 1980s and 1990s, leaving her feeling insecure and with intense self doubt. She was expected to remove the mole on her face. She overcame self doubt by refusing to give in to industry demands, facing her fears and turning towards self-acceptance. She embraced her mole and flaunted it proudly

– not knowing that it would become her trademark – and the confidence that she gained from her experience would prepare her to fight the imposter syndrome that would raise its ugly head every now and then during her career.

Cindy had chosen an industry where models were exploited and pressured into doing unpleasant things, and despite all of the glitz and glamour, as soon as the lights went out on the ramp, they were replaced by the darkness of anxiety, fear, rejection, isolation, insecurities, doubts, guilt, and shame. But she kept her focus and stood her ground through the challenges, all the while prioritizing professionalism over an easy way up. When faced with glass barriers, she transitioned from being a model to a media personality, venturing into brand endorsements and acting.

As one of the most photographed women in the world, she was under constant scrutiny for her looks. Her personal life and ageing process was subject to harsh public speculation, and even though she may have had sleepless nights over this, she chose to gracefully present ageing in women through her own example, rejecting shame about getting older. She launched her own business ventures in the beauty industry, something completely unheard of at the turn of the century. Coupled with her resilience and adaptability, she built a successful business empire and a well-balanced family life. This made her into a role model for many young women in the industry, and she also used her voice to speak out on industry issues and inspire young women to aim for balance, grace, and confidence.

Her life is an example of not giving into internal insecurities and external industry expectations, and instead overcoming these with confidence and grace, to maintain a sense of perspective and personal identity in a fiercely competitive world.

> *"If you let the industry define you, you lose yourself. You have to define you."*

While the demons are many, the ways to fight them are few. These emotions hover over us all the time, like a swarm of bees, and we never know which ones are going to sting. The best way to protect ourselves and to cope is to use a "bee veil" of techniques, including the theory of Aligned Perfection.

## The Theory of Aligned Perfection

Perfection, or near perfection, is the target we give ourselves, as we want to ensure that we do our best. It is usually not something that comes from outside. Perfection in how we commit to our role, our actions, decisions, and so on is a good target, but perfection in what we want to achieve in our goals – perfect outcomes, perfect work, perfect life, and perfect balance – is a definitive way of setting ourselves up for failure. Excellent work-life balance is not impossible, but in order to achieve that, it is imperative that we be willing to change our mindset around perfection.

After struggling for years with this goal of being perfect all the time at everything I do, I developed the theory of Aligned Perfection. As high-achieving women, we keep giving ourselves goals that are big, and we tell ourselves we have to do everything right, everything perfectly, to be able to reach the perfect goal in perfect timing, while having a perfect family and finally have a perfect work-life balance.

After years of beating myself up over failures and imperfect outcomes, I turned inwards to seek guidance. After years of meditation, spirituality, introspection, journaling, and listening to motivational speakers and working with coaches, I came to realize that I need to work on my mindset in a handful of different ways. Giving up perfection felt like an unfulfilling, passion-draining project, and so I discovered that I need to adjust the mindset around perfection. I align my perfection now with these principles.

- Perfect work life balance is not an outcome or a goal – it is a means to the goal.
- If I can't stop the pursuit of perfection, then I must seek perfection in action, not in outcome.
- The flaws of society are not in my control, but my own flaws are.
- Not all flaws need to be fixed; some need to be embraced.
- I must align my perfection with what I can control (my actions and decisions), and remove it completely from the outcome or the result that is not in my control.

## Taking Action:

Embracing the theory of Aligned Perfection is the mindset shift that can take some practice and some time. You will need constant reminders to yourself, and where possible, having a buy in from your spouse and children. Put reminders in multiple places – screensavers, notebooks, diaries, journals, vision boards, etc.

**Once the internal barometer is calibrated to the new mindset, the day-to-day actions will be small tasks and be a little bit easier to manage. Some weapons to hold in our arsenal include:**

1. Labelling feelings and emotions, and bringing in logic to squash them.
2. Reframing guilt by focusing on values rather than perfection.
3. Building our self-confidence enough to be bold amidst our vulnerabilities.
4. Connecting with our tribe – there are many women in the same shoes as us, and we can support each other through meaningful connection and by being vulnerable. Connect with other empowering and supportive women and build our advisor or mentor network.
5. Prioritizing self care, and things that make us happy.
6. Learning to ask for help, support, guidance, suggestion, opinion, and motivation.
7. Keep your why at the forefront of everything.

RULE 9

# STAY AUTHENTIC

For one day the mask will become unbearable and fall to reveal the unbearable sight of an eroded soul, and only the truly authentic will survive to tell the tale.

Authenticity is one trait that is often trivialized in many ways, and in its true sense is not being valued as an important attribute for leaders. Being authentic means being true to yourself and aligning yourself with your inner core – raw, unfiltered, and real – and this is not a quality that is rewarded by a world that has certain set norms and expectations and considers it better to conform to them. Most people bury their authenticity and put on a mask, or several masks, in order to conform and be accepted.

Being accepted is a comfort zone that all humans seek, even if it comes at the cost of losing a piece of ourselves along the way. Taking on the persona that the world expects to see for too long makes you forget who you truly are. The foundation for your achievements is then based on the weak poles of the false image you have created for yourself and for the world to see. It is an easy path forward, with minimum resistance and easy acceptance, but how much of you will be truly you by the time you reach the summit?

> *"The place you thought was yours, was actually only for the mask. The space that the maskless make, is theirs forever to keep and revel."*

Meaning isn't found – it's created by how honestly you live.

Staying true to ourselves, accepting ourselves completely, and aligning our actions with who we truly are, is an act of liberation. When we stop shrinking ourselves to fit the mould, we allow ourselves to expand into the growth we desire and that our soul desires. As women, in our circle of life, our soul's purpose or our soul's desires matter way more than they matter for most men, and authenticity is the way of fulfilling it honestly. Authenticity brings many rewards, although that path is ridden with discomfort, difficulties and resistance. To be aware of the pros and the cons of authenticity is important in order to stay the track, *not* to make a decision whether it is the right path.

### Authenticity brings a sense of purpose.

There are two types of people: ones who know their purpose and ones who don't. If we know our purpose, defining it clearly makes it easier to identify our soul's path. Pursuing this path takes many different skills and strengths, most importantly the ability to be true to ourselves. Brutal honesty is the compass that guides us on our path, and authenticity is the navigation app that guides us to walk the *right* path. Every choice and every decision, no matter how small, becomes sacred when it reflects our truth.

### Authenticity grounds us in self-respect and trust.

When we follow our inner compass, when we embrace our authenticity, we build trust in ourselves, and that helps deepen our self-respect. Faith in ourselves is the biggest gift, because that is the foundation of our identity. When we no longer seek validation, we are whole, and everything else that we achieve are external, accumulated things that don't define us. Who we are is the only thing that no one can take away from us, and who we are is the courage that pulls us through the unavoidable challenges we face in our lives.

### Authenticity gives meaning to our relationships.

As we embrace authenticity, we will automatically lose people who do not resonate with us. Those who care only to conform to be accepted by society and peers will drop out, and people who align with authenticity will be attracted to us. These relationships are more meaningful and less transactional because we accept each other for who we are and not for the versions that they want us to be.

### Authenticity dissolves negative emotions, like guilt and shame.

When we are authentic, we own our life, we own our story. We do not seek validation or acceptance from others. Our trust is in our values, our beliefs, and our abilities, and we own our scars and our losses. We become capable of identifying our vulnerabilities and our imperfections, and that is a gateway to healing. When we accept ourselves, we melt away the shame and guilt.

### Authenticity creates alignment.

When our values, efforts, thoughts, and actions align every single time, we are being true to ourselves. It is the power that enables us to make decisions and act in ways that are consistent with our core beliefs and principles. Authenticity is not an action to take sometimes and to omit the other times; it is a way of being.

When every part of our being aligns, life flows more freely. There may be more resistance to it outside, but internally there is less friction. Less burnout and less pretense give us more energy to pursue our path. When we stop being who we're *supposed* to be, and embrace who we truly are, the energy of the Universe flows through us unhindered, aligning our being with our purpose.

> *"The privilege of a lifetime is to become who you truly are."*
> **– Carl Jung**

## Golda Meir

Born in Kiev, Russia (present day Ukraine) in 1898, Golda Meir was Israel's first and only female prime minister, and one of the most formidable women in modern political history. She is considered to be the original "Iron Lady," and her early years were cloaked in poverty and antisemitic violence. Finding herself facing cultural pressure to marry young, she fled home at 14 to pursue further education in the United States. A fiercely independent mindset pushed her towards activism, and she joined the Zionist Youth movement with the gallant dream of building a Jewish homeland.

Considered to be a brash decision at the time, she moved with her husband to the British Mandate (present-day Israel) in 1921, leaving the comforts and the safety of the country that gave her refuge. She found her true calling in the establishment of an independent Jewish state, and acceded to the grueling, primitive male-dominated life of *kibbutz*. She was drawn by her passion, and not swayed by the comforts of life she had access to in the US. It took great strength to see her sacrifices belittled and her political opinions ignored by the male Zionist leaders of the Jewish trade union and the Labour Zionist movement. Her unwavering commitment to Zionism, along with the ability to think strategically and be an influential public speaker and negotiator, won her eventual favor. Her idealism and authenticity melted away even the harshest skepticism from her compatriots.

Defying British immigration quotas for Jews during the second world war, she resolutely helped smuggle Jewish refugees from war-torn Europe into British Palestine. Her ignorance of the risk of being arrested for doing so often seemed reckless.

Her unshakeable drive for a Jewish state, and a profound conviction that it was her soul's purpose to do so peacefully, justified her secret travels to meet King Abdullah of Jordan, in an attempt to avoid war. When diplomacy failed, she dove right in to turn the tide of the Israel-Arab war, and traveled to US to rally support and $50 million in funding, both of which proved critical for Israel's survival during its War of Independence against its Arab neighbours.

When the state of Israel was finally established in May 1948, Golda was appointed Israel's first ambassador to the Soviet Union, during the tumultuous times of Stalin's rise in the post-war era. Her upfront diplomacy style was unconventional for the job, but nevertheless, she was successful in establishing a diplomatic relationship and enhancing Israel's legitimacy on the international stage.

In spite of being one of the 24 people who signed the document of Israel's Declaration of Independence in 1948, her political journey was not devoid of hurdles. She climbed the shaky ladder with relentless determination, serving as Labour minister first, then foreign minister, and finally prime minister in 1969. During her tenure, Israel faced constant security threats, acts of terrorism, and the Yom Kippur War, an armed conflict with the coalition of the Arab nations under the leadership of Egypt and Syria. In an attempt to maintain peace in the region and to have continued support from Europe and the US, she decided not to pre-emptively attack the Arab forces, despite the knowledge of the troops. She rallied US support for the war, which led to an eventual victory for Israel.

Although her quick strategic decision-making may have been the primary reason for the victory, the victory itself, and her ability to bring in American support for Israel, was overlooked, and she was criticized for intelligence lapses and for the resultant loss of Israeli lives. An inquiry into the government's failure to act proactively cleared her of any wrongdoing, and yet she chose to resign from office and claim responsibility for the losses. Her act of stepping down in such a manner was a rare act of humility and idyllic to her national solidarity.

Golda Meir became a global symbol of female leadership long before feminism was mainstream. She did this in the face of diplomacy and that of war-through her steel resolve and her authenticity in her goals and her values, her compassion, and her fearless leadership.

*"But above all, in order to be, never try to seem."*

**– Albert Camus**

Choosing to be truly and unapologetically yourself is a difficult journey, and it involves identifying and connecting with your true self and resisting the pressure to be someone else. The preeminent requisition for authenticity is self-awareness, which requires us to burrow deep within ourselves to understand our values, our principles, our strengths, and our weaknesses, and to do so with complete and brutal honesty.

But that is not the only difficult part. It takes unshakeable confidence to consciously decide to be yourself in a world that constantly expects you to be someone else. The unspoken rules of compliance and complicit silence dominate some personal – and all professional – environments. Those who speak up and refuse to play by the rules are not welcome.

Being authentic triggers a sense of insecurity in people around us. When you are real, when you are authentic, the stark contrast of falsehood, pretense, and conformity around you becomes extremely obvious, and the exposure does not go down well for those who have chosen to play the game and compromise their integrity, values, and principles.

Forsaking their truth for comfort, security and approval from others, they have built their lives and careers around these beliefs. When you take the radical decision to speak your truth, it challenges their perceptions and their beliefs, exposing their glaring inability to be honest with themselves. This does not go down well, not because they think they are right, but because they know they are wrong, and, out of fear of losing everything that they have built for themselves, they cannot change that. They see in you what they could be but choose not to be.

Authenticity is not a virtue that the world rewards, and it takes courage and conviction to squash the urge to conform to ideas that contradict one's beliefs. The moment you decide to embody your authentic self and your presence reminds people of what they have been avoiding in the name of what needs to be done. They are reminded of all the dreams they have abandoned, all the times they have silenced their voices. This confrontation with their truth is what makes them uncomfortable, and thereby puts you in harm's way. Those who choose the comfort of acceptance over integrity and authenticity are painfully aware of your courage to embrace authenticity, and they project their insecurity onto you by labeling you arrogant or difficult.

As much as it is difficult to understand this concept of diverted blame, it is crucial to not play small. Author Tara Mohr, in her book *Playing Big*, says that when people call you too much or too intense for being your true, authentic self, it is not because you are wrong, but because labelling you as wrong makes it easier for them to accept themselves. But resist the urge to play small, resist the urge to live as per what is expected out of you, to act and conform to the expectations. Playing small is exhausting, because you have to constantly shrink yourself to fit into the mould they have designed for you. Playing big and embodying your authenticity, on the other hand, is liberating.

Authenticity is also about the courage to walk alone, to make sacrifices on that road and to constantly swim against the tide. When people see someone embracing their authenticity, it makes them question why they are not brave enough to live the way you live. Some will get inspired and embrace their own truths, and it's never too late to do so. Some will mock you for being foolish enough to think that authenticity gets you anywhere in life. And some will try to pull you down, blinded by envy that you could do what they could not.

When they can't match you, they reject you, because you, just by being yourself, just by existing, are an unbearable reminder to them that they've betrayed themselves. Those who have chosen to numb their authenticity have been able to open up an easy pathway for them to find success and favour in community and in industry. They are terrified, because they could choose to be authentic but chose not to. By playing big, you make them face their truth, and they resent you for it. By being true to yourself, you break the norms, upend the social fabric, and fall through the holes to land alone on a difficult pathway.

Step into that discomfort, embrace the resistance, and stand firmly in who you are. By resisting the pressure to be someone you're not and choosing to act in a way that aligns with your true self, you are changing the world around you, unconsciously forcing them to look outside the illusions that they have built for themselves. Those who do not have the stomach for truth, and don't have the courage to be themselves, distance themselves from you. While you may be left feeling alone, it is actually a good thing to let the inauthentic drift away by themselves. Its only when you make room in your life, that similarly authentic people with aligned energies will enter.

> *"If you don't know who you truly are, you'll never know what you really want."*
>
> **– Roy T. Bennett**

### Priyanka Chopra

Priyanka Chopra's journey as a young girl from a military background to winning the title of Miss India and then Miss World, then onward to Bollywood and to Hollywood, is also a journey of ambition, self-acceptance, and authenticity. Now, a very powerful force to be reckoned with globally, the challenges she faced were endless.

While she describes the winning of Miss India title as something that she was expecting, the title of Miss World in 2000 catapulted Priyanka onto the global stage. Not giving into the pressures of the pageants, she stayed true to her roots and asked for what she thought was right. This encouraged her to stand her ground when she entered Bollywood, the world of Indian cinema.

She faced extreme pressure and unruly demands in this male-dominated industry, but she held onto authenticity as her source of courage. Whether it was being ousted from projects or being typecast into certain roles, Priyanka faced doubts and felt boxed in by the industry pressures. Her family, which has been her pillar of strength, kept her grounded and authentic, and encouraged her to pursue her dreams, despite resistance from industry veterans. Crying out her fears and dejections at night, she continued with the same determination each morning. Her resilience and hard work paid off as she won awards and recognition for staggering roles she played in unconventional Bollywood movies.

Frustration and ambition drove Priyanka to make a decision to explore opportunities in the US entertainment industry. It was a conscious decision to eject herself from the mould given to her by Bollywood, and to grow and expand in an even bigger and global entertainment industry, a move that most did not anticipate. At a time when some people around her expected her to leave the industry altogether, she left, only to enter an even bigger stage.

She strategically signed up with one of the top talent agencies in Hollywood, resisting temptation and rejecting the typical "Indian girl" roles, thereby defying norms as an outsider in the industry. She stayed true to her perspective and her vision of herself, and when offers didn't knock on her door, she attempted to open the doors through music.

She produced a few singles, and though they received a lukewarm response, the action did help her gain visibility and forge connections within the industry. Being dismissed time and again as just a beauty queen from India, she had to work hard to adapt to an American accent and to learn cultural nuances so that she could become relatable enough to be considered for mainstream roles in Hollywood.

Relentlessly putting up a brave face against repeated skepticism for years, she landed her breakthrough role in the TV series *Quantico*. It was a landmark moment for a South Asian actor to be the lead actor on an American TV show. Her performance, and the accolades she received, were remarkable in ways more than we can perceive. She was also the first South Asian actress to win the People's Choice award for her performance, and she paved the way for other South Asian actors to enter mainstream Hollywood. This recognition opened the doors to major studios in Hollywood, and since then, she has been unstoppable.

Her portfolio boasts both Oscar-nominated films and meaningful roles close to her heart.

Time and again on her motivational podcasts, she speaks up about fighting against people's expectations of her and finding her rightful opportunities by denying those who asked her to play small and expanding her horizons by staying true to herself. She speaks up about the bullying or resistance she faced at different stages of her life and career, and how staying authentic helped her stay grounded and focused on her purpose. Through her work and her voice, she inspires people who aspire to break across cultures, industries and borders.

From being a well-renowned actor to starting a production company – Purple Pebble Pictures – to supporting regional Indian cinema and championing diverse voices globally, she has inadvertently become a bridge between East and West. She is a role model for aspiring actors of color, and she uses her fame to advocate for children's rights and girls' education globally. Staying authentic helped her maintain sanity and maintain focus, and empowered her to assert her worth.

Today she is a well-respected actor and producer in the global entertainment industry, and a champion for various important causes. She is a true example of how authenticity is the most powerful tool in your kit. The journey may be long and hard, filled with challenges, but if you have the mettle, you can break barriers.

*"Be yourself; everyone else is already taken."*

**– Oscar Wilde**

While it is possible for some of us to live authentically, without thought or effort, most people are conditioned to prioritize compliance over integrity, and have been convinced that success comes from playing along and silencing their voice. Authenticity challenges this belief and proves it wrong. Those who can hear their inner voices nagging at them are being called to embrace their authenticity. Their facades fading, their masks cracking, they become painfully aware of the signs that the acceptance that they have gained, that the success that they have achieved, was never truly meant for them, but instead for the sculpted version that they wanted the world to see. The choices, then, are limited between continuing to shrink to fit into the box you have been given, or showing the courage to embody authenticity without fearing the consequences.

### Authenticity is about overcoming fear.

Other than loneliness, authenticity brings many hurdles, the blame game, being outcast, difficulties in your pathway, and manufactured legal or other complaints. But instead of looking for short-term happiness, it is wiser to choose long-term peace. Slowly but surely, it helps us align our life with the Higher Power.

### Authenticity is about conscience.

The lower the conscientiousness, the easier it is to stay away from authenticity. When we truly accept ourselves and stay true to our values and principles, we are feeding our conscience as well. Highly conscientious people are going to find it easier to be authentic and to adapt, irrespective of what the perceived demands of the situation are.

### Authenticity is about prioritizing inner peace.

The choice to step out of the collective mould, and to stop taking directions from unwritten rules, will not seem easy, but know that it is the right one. Authenticity brings us to a place of inner peace, because we are being ourselves, operating in sync with the rhythm of the Universe.

We raise our vibrations to the same frequency as that of the Universe simply by being true to ourselves, and life flows.

### Authenticity is about listening to oneself.

If you don't know how to be authentic, or if you feel that you are authentic but are unsure, it is because the culture, the self-help books, and the business development tools all teach us to be compliant and gain approval, even if it comes at the cost of integrity.

The first step is listening deeply to ourselves about what our true essence is and connecting with nature and our deepest core to identify what matters to us the most. We must identify our values and principles and bring them to the forefront so they are always clearly visible.

### Authenticity means embracing imperfection.

It's only when we are able to face our flaws that we can evolve into authenticity. Authenticity is a balance of humility and gratitude, and being aware that there is so much we don't know, as well as what we already know is also enough.

### Authenticity is about recognizing our wholeness.

It's about being fully and constantly alive – *not* in episodes. It is only when we are that way in every moment of our lives that we truly live and connect with others from a deeper level.

### The Glory of Authenticity

Authenticity in all its glory is not perfection – it's wholeness. And while there are many challenges on this uneven road, it is still a highly rewarding journey to take. To be authentic is to live from your center, not your surface, and whether it's in a quiet whisper or a bold roar, authenticity is a sacred rebellion in a world that often rewards imitation. And in those narrow windy tough roads of authenticity, we find ourselves.

It is liberating for our energies and our life force to have an open field of honesty. As much as it is messy, it is a beautiful journey to take. Authenticity is magnetic to other authentic people, and it is magnetic to the manifestations of our dreams. Authenticity is about the courage to choose truth over approval, integrity over convenience, and wholeness over image, and it leads our soul to a meaningful, liberated, and aligned life. When we work from this place of authenticity, we connect deeper, play bigger, create grander, and live fuller. It is only when we stop hiding behind masks that life itself stops hiding from us.

*"My truth is my power. I don't have to perform, hide, or prove – I only have to be."*

## Taking Action:

This is one of those rules that has no real steps. The whole chapter is to imbibe the meaning of authenticity and then embark on our journey. The journey to our authenticity is unique to each one of us. It is not an act of doing; it is a way of being. Authenticity begins with being fully in touch with ourselves- physically, mentally, emotionally, spiritually.

1. **Meditate:** Do the AUM chant 21 times (again, A from the base of the stomach, U from the chest and M from the throat) every day as a source of strength and courage from the Universe. Feel the vibrations created by the AUM chanting in every part of your body, starting at the top of your head, down to your face and neck. Trace it down to your chest, lungs, abdomen, pelvis. Trace it down your shoulder, arm and fingertips, and down your hips, thighs, knees and legs and toes. Feel the vibration in every cell of your body, and flowing through the blood vessels. In doing so you connect with who you truly are, physically, mentally, spiritually.
2. **Nourish:** Eat healthy, drink enough water, nourish the body that supports your being.
3. **Nurture:** Provide your body and mind with the fuel it needs. Connect with nature, go out for walks, workout, find a physical activity that you enjoy.

RULE 10

# KNOW BAD DAYS ARE REAL

In the midst of the wildest storms, will you find your deepest strength.

Imagine you go through all the steps we discussed previously. You go through the efforts of identifying and defining your goals and you learn how to pick the right battles and make the tough decisions. You focus on your priorities, and you learn to trust in yourself. Imagine you have developed mastery over how to seize the opportunity when it presents itself, and to stand your ground, all the while maintaining your authenticity. Now what? Everything should fall into place and you should be able to command the world and achieve your goals the way want to, right?

I wish life was so simple. We all do. But its only now that you will recognize that bad days are real. Such is life – we can prepare all we want, we can pray and hope all we like, but in the end, life is unpredictable, and this unpredictability is what makes life beautiful. The blend of magical realism and reality is what makes life beautiful and enigmatic. Japanese author Haruki Murakami, through his writing, touches upon this essence of life.

> *"...And once the storm is over, you won't remember how you made it through, how you managed to survive. You won't even be sure whether the storm is really over. But one thing is certain: when you come out of the storm, you won't be the same person who walked in. That's what this storm is all about."*
>
> **– Haruki Murakami**

Just because things can go wrong, just because there will be tears along the way, doesn't mean we should stop living. We have to concentrate on the here and now, because if we keep speculating on what can go wrong, we won't be able to take the first step, or any step whatsoever. Instead of going through a very detailed analysis of all the things that can go wrong, it is sometimes best to just take the leap of faith. On one end of the path is fear and the other is faith – and somewhere in between those lines lies the truth.

Worry is the end of action. As if our brains already don't have enough much to deal with, we often focus on every possibility of every adversity. Fear then, is bound to paralyze our ability to put in the right effort and to take the right action. If we rely on the theory of Aligned Perfection, if we only focus on things in our control, if we only focus on our efforts and our actions and our decisions, and the rest to the Universe to figure out, the difficulties and the hurdles will eventually dissipate.

> *"I judge you unfortunate because you have never lived through misfortune. You have passed through life without an opponent – no one can ever know what you are capable of, not even you."*
>
> **– Seneca**

We are born on this earth to help humanity evolve, and one of the ways to do so is through experience. Our tough times help us find our deepest strengths, and it's only when we face an adversity that we look inwards to seek the courage and the fortitude to battle. It is here that we can build our mettle and bring forth the hidden superpowers that we will need on our journey ahead. While the weak will give up, the strong ones will gather all that valour, bundle it up together, and move ahead with even greater force.

Sometimes we may face small challenges, like not being selected or the door not opening, or having a sick child to attend to on the day of the most important meeting. At other times, these could be a little more tormenting, like discrimination or being robbed of an opportunity without a good reason, or having to prove oneself over and over again. The challenges could be soul-crushing, mentally devastating, or take a physical toll, like facing a huge failure in spite of tremendous amount of preparation, losing your designation due to a false accusation, or even personal loss.

We can never be prepared for every single one of those, but the first step is to remind ourselves that there is no other way forward than going through this experience and learning the lesson it is here to teach us. Over time, we learn to identify a challenge as a lesson and not as a hurdle. It may not be easy at first, but it is a point of view that brings objectivity and eliminates self-blame and guilt. Once we get over the guilt, shame, and other negative feelings, this objective point of view will give us more clarity about how we need to tackle the challenge.

## Kalpana Chawla

Kalpana Chawla, the first woman of Indian origin to go to space, was also the first woman to die in space. Born in Karnal, Haryana, in 1962, a time and place where girls were often discouraged from pursuing careers in science or aviation, Chawla was born to challenge societal norms. While her family was by no means wealthy, they supported her education and put all their resources to that end. They saw the curiosity of the young girl who would draw airplanes and talk about soaring high above the skies.

Graduating with a degree in aerospace engineering, a male-dominated field, was a very unusual choice for girls in rural India at the time. She was met with skepticism not just from people close to her, but also from fellow students and teachers and professors. Not letting herself get distracted from her goals, she moved to the US and got her first master's degree in aerospace engineering from University of Texas.

While that enabled her growth in the aerospace industry, she recognized the deficiencies that could hold her back from going to space, so she got her second master's degree, as well as PhD in aerospace engineering from University of Colorado. Pursuing advanced degrees in aerospace, and moving to the United States, took massive leaps of faith, considerable financial strain. and cultural adjustment. In adapting to a new society with different social and educational norms, it was not unusual for an immigrant at the time to face cultural and social isolation and language barriers.

In 1988, Chawla was hired by NASA as a research scientist. Working out of the Ames Research Centre in California, she studied computational fluid dynamics and complex airflow simulations around the aircraft. The study helped her compute the intricate airflow patterns surrounding an aircraft, crucial for designing safer and more fuel-efficient aircraft. She also did studies on vertical takeoffs and landings, thereby reducing the amount of space needed for runways. Post her stint at Ames, she continued her research at Overset Methods as vice president and research scientist focusing on aerodynamic optimization techniques. In 1995, she was selected by NASA to join the Johnson Space Centre as an astronaut candidate in the fifteenth group of astronauts. She underwent extensive physical and mental training, including learning to cope under pressure and in isolation, to work as a team and operate spacecraft, to conduct experiments in space using the robotic arm, and to handle emergencies of every possible nature.

STS-87 Columbia was the fourth U.S microgravity payload flight, focused on experiments designed to study how the weightless environment of space affects various physical processes, and the observations of the sun's outer atmospheric layers. Kalpana Chawla spent 30 days in space on that mission.

As an immigrant woman of color in aerospace, she had to constantly prove her capabilities in a field dominated by American men in order to be selected for the mission. During that crucial mission, the well-prepared astronaut was appointed as the mission specialist, and while the mission successfully completed its objectives, and Chawla's work with the robotic arm contributed to the success of the experiments, a malfunction of the Spartan satellite led to an investigation into Chawla's role and responsibility of the malfunction.

The 252 orbits made around the earth, a span of 6.5 million miles in 376 hours and 34 minutes, brought her the joy of living her dream, and yet the malfunction shook her belief in herself. While the NASA investigation cleared her of fault, the scrutiny was emotionally challenging and confidence draining.

*"Most of the important things in the world have been accomplished by people who have kept on trying when there seemed to be no hope at all."*

**– Dale Carnegie**

She persevered through the tough times, rebuilt trust with her colleagues, and all the while kept the flame alive. She was selected for her second space mission, STS-107, to conduct experiments in biology and physics, and went through another round of intense physical, technical, and psychological preparation. The mission faced several delays, some due to scheduling conflicts, others due to more serious life-threatening issues with the body of the shuttle, and finally took flight in January 2003.

As Kalpana Chawla and the other astronauts boarded the Space shuttle Columbia and took off, no one knew that this would be the last time these seven astronauts set foot on earth. The catastrophic disintegration of the ship during re-entry into the earth's atmosphere, tragically ended the mission, as well as the lives of all those onboard abruptly.

The Columbia Accident Investigation Board (CAIB) revealed that the disaster was caused by a piece of foam insulation that broke off from the external fuel tank during launch, damaging the orbiter's thermal protection system on the left wing. This damage allowed superheated air to penetrate the wing structure, leading to its disintegration during re-entry. The cause of this devastating explosion was ironically tied to the research that Chawla did on airflow and safety and integrity of aircrafts and shuttle bodies. The CAIB's report also highlighted systemic issues within NASA, including cultural and managerial shortcomings that contributed to the accident, and led to a wave of significant changes in NASA's safety protocols and procedures.

> *"Every adversity has the seed of an equivalent or greater benefit."*
>
> **– Napoleon Hill**

One of the most prominent cultural shifts was for NASA employees to have the remains of Columbia visible as a reminder of their jobs to keep the astronauts safe, a move that may have been a major contributor to the safe return of Barry Willmore and Sunita Williams Earth in early 2025, after an overextended stay of nine months at the International Space Station.

Kalpana Chawla was a trailblazer in her field, and her life exemplified courage and perseverance through tough times. Her heroism is in not amplifying the risks and dangers that come along the way of bold dreams and overcoming the odds of gender bias, cultural displacement, and institutional hurdles patiently, quietly, and with grit. While being critically aware of the risk of losing her life, she took firm steps towards her dreams. While her life inspires many young women today, her death is what provoked introspection in a massively powerful global organization like NASA and brought about colossal changes within the core of the organization.

> *"Opportunities to find deeper powers within ourselves come when life seems most challenging."*
>
> **– Joseph Campbell**

Life is not what we expect – it is made up of the most unexpected and the most riveting twists and turns. It brings along challenges and hurdles to test our resolve, to test how badly we really want something. Everybody can have a dream, but one difference between those who achieve their goals and those who don't is perseverance. When we face insurmountable challenges, the Universe is testing us, to see if we have built the mettle, to see if we are ready, and to see if we are truly willing. Sometimes small inconveniences may show up along the way, but when a major hurdle blocks our way, it is more often than not just before the culmination of our dreams and our goals. Being patient on the journey and adhering ourselves to action, rather than a quick result, is an important skill to learn in this day and age of instant gratification.

Having the inner strengths of patience and perseverance may also not be enough during certain challenges, and we may need to seek out mentors, friends, business coaches, or a tribe to seek guidance. No matter what it takes, go inwards or outwards to seek support, strength, and guidance, and to stay positive during tough times. A positive mindset is the first requirement of any action, small or bold. Imbibing the qualities and strengths from our close tribe or from distant role models by learning and reading about them is crucial on this journey to our goals.

> *"Success is to be measured, not so much by the position that one has reached in life as by the obstacles which he has overcome."*
>
> **– Booker T. Washington**

## Rosalind Franklin

British chemist and X-ray crystallographer Rosalind Franklin did some pioneering research that was critical to understanding the molecular structures at the core of humanity. While her scientific breakthroughs in identifying the structures of DNA, RNA, and viruses was pivotal to the understanding of genetic material, immunity and inheritance of traits, her research on coal and graphite opened up the doorways to many industrial applications. Her groundbreaking research spanned across several industries and impacted many new age advances of the 20th century. Her determination in the face of systemic gender bias, and her disciplined scientific rigor in the midst of extreme professional injustice throughout her career, provides just a glimpse into her perseverance and strength of character.

Born in London to a prominent and affluent Jewish family of scholars, she was highly intelligent and was encouraged to pursue academic excellence. As the Nazis marched across Europe, she continued her studies while also closely following the war, debating British foreign policy in letters to her family and volunteering as an air raid warden. She pursued science and scored a graduate degree in physical chemistry from Cambridge in 1941, a time when there was no provision to extend full degrees to women. During her time at Cambridge, she stood up to inequality and demanded equal treatment for men and women. Her research and PhD during World War II on the structure and properties of coal enabled the creation of gas masks used during the war. Discovering the ability of activated charcoal and its porosity to be used as filters proved lifesaving for millions during the war, providing an effective barrier against poisonous gases.

The years ensuing World War II were steeped in recovery, division, and post-destruction transformation. Amidst political realignments and rising communism in Europe, Franklin moved to Paris to work at the Laboratoire Central des Services Chimiques de l'Etat, where she enjoyed the freedom to pursue her interests and mastered the technique of X-ray crystallography. With the technology of X-ray diffraction – a method that determines the arrangements of atoms in solids and crystals – she became engrossed in revealing the structures of different carbons, thereby laying the foundation for new industrial uses of carbon and the development of heat-resistant materials.

As recently as the 1950s, female scientists were treated as second-class citizens and were susceptible to hostile work environments. In the post-war era, scientists across the globe raced to discover the structure of DNA, as biology was a solace for the recovering world. Franklin, being an international authority on carbons and X-ray diffraction, was invited by the King's College in London to apply the technology to identify the structure of DNA and other biological structures.

Franklin worked for hours in a non-conducive environment, in her relentless pursuit of this cause. She faced discrimination and marginalization by male colleagues, professors and the institution itself. The academia and scientific communities at the time were misogynist and barred women from entering even the lunchrooms, let alone the rooms where decisions were made. Her confident demeanor was often labeled as "difficult" or "abrasive," labels that were reserved only for women scientists, but considered normal, approved and well-accepted if it was a male scientist.

While being profoundly unhappy at the injustice, she devoted her time instead to building the right microscope and camera for her work on DNA. At such an opprobrious time for female scientists, despite her undeniable expertise in her field she received little institutional support, and was often implicitly told that science was not mean for women. She was given the designation of a "research associate" at King's College, a derogatory title for her stature, and the one that deprived her of any authority – even though she was leading the research.

This misguided title created repeated misunderstandings with Maurice Wilkins, her colleague, who implied that Franklin's role was to assist him in his research, and also that he owned the rights to any work done by her. She routinely clashed with Maurice, which led to tension in the lab. No one will ever know for sure if these were the reasons behind Maurice sharing the historical and groundbreaking "Photo 51" with fellow scientists James Watson and Francis Crick.

*"Opportunities to find deeper powers within ourselves come when life seems most challenging."*

**– Joseph Campbell**

The assertive, uncompromising Jewish female scientist was deceived by the male-dominated scientific community on many levels, but what is more remarkable is that she ignored the attitude of her surroundings aside and stayed focused as she suspended a tiny DNA fiber, with the thickness of a strand of hair, and bombarded it with an X-ray beam for 100 hours of exposure under carefully controlled relative humidity. When these rays were diffracted by the electrons in the atoms of the DNA fiber, they produced a pattern on a photographic plate, which was "Photo 51."

Never had X-ray crystallography been put to such deft or momentous use, and yet it is tainted in ignominy. The male scientists, who unabashedly took the photo to replicate it into a model and publish it in scientific journals, failed to mention Franklin's contribution not only in their published article but also when they were awarded the Nobel Prize for the DNA structure. These would have been probably pardoned by history as mindless, dimwitted decisions, if it weren't for James Watson painting Franklin in an unflattering and dismissive light, calling her names and criticizing her personality rather than praising her brilliance.

The men in academia had demonstrated their insecurity and entitlement. In some industries, the trend still continues.

*"If you can't fly then run, if you can't run then walk, if you can't walk then crawl, but whatever you do you have to keep moving forward."*

**– Dr Martin Luther King, Jr**

Invited by her mentor Dr Bernal, world's leading crystallographer, she moved to Birkbeck College's Biomolecular Research Lab to do research on viruses. The resentment and trampling attitude from King's College followed her there, instructing her to terminate all her work on DNA. Rosalind had already moved on to more impactful work, and her focus was on contributing to science, irrespective of the credit coming her way or not.

The overshadowing of her role in the DNA structure discovery led to decades of underappreciation of her contributions. She focused on research and scientific presentations, often being the only woman in the room, and despite her spectacular contributions and pioneering research, the funding, the support and the status eluded her. When she was offered a contract by the Agricultural Research Council, without the title of principal researcher, and without an appropriate reimbursement, she showed humility and focused on science. She thrived on scientific collaborations and secured funding from National institute of Health in the US, basic needs as a scientist denied to her in the UK.

Franklin was sometimes admired, mostly resented, and always sidelined during her lifetime. She was subjected to posthumous obscurity for decades. And while misappropriation of her work at King's College was the most despicable admonishment of her life's work, the smaller social and cultural and institutional day-to-day belittling was probably what bothered her more.

> *"Tough situations build strong people in the end."*
>
> **– Roy T Bennett**

Despite the obstacles, the unjust social norms, institutional biases, and professional rivalries of the time, her razor-sharp focus on her contributions laid the foundation for one of the greatest scientific breakthroughs of the 20th century. Working through her cancer diagnosis, she exemplified courage, determination, and dedication during her short life span of 38 years. During her lifetime, she was not accorded the well-deserved acknowledgement for her scientific contributions, and she desultorily became one of the most famous archetypes of the larger issue in society – the erasure of women's achievements in man's world.

> *"No man is more unhappy than he who never faces adversity. For he is not permitted to prove himself."*
>
> **– Seneca**

All great stories, all inspiring journeys, and all accomplished people prove that challenges are part and parcel of growth. There is no growth without challenges, and professional adversity for an individual can bring about profound personal growth. At times, personal adversity may also play a crucial role in bringing a massive societal or cultural change.

Challenges are here to test our resolve, to test how badly we really want something. Whether we get it during this lifetime, or posthumously like these women we talked about, there is something about the role of individual achievements in collective humanity that we may never fathom. Irrcspective of when we accomplish what we set out to, we have to keep moving forward with a strong resolve.

Challenges makes life interesting, and overcoming them makes life meaningful. Every day may not be good, but there's something good in every day. Focus on the good, no matter how small, because at the end of the day, what doesn't kill you makes you stronger. Treat these bad days as a challenging HIIT and circuit day for your mind – stay calm and focus on your next step, and know that it will end. For those not shattered by the present are not frightened by the future.

For those not shattered by the present are not frightened by the future.

## Taking Action:

1. **Evening Meditation:** Inhale, exhale, repeat, focusing on physical relaxation. Then inhale, exhale, repeat focusing on mental relaxation. Imagine yourself in a forest: calm, green, peaceful, beautiful. You can smell the trees and the moist earth. You can hear the wind rustle in the trees, and the birds sing in the distance. You can hear a waterfall close by. Walk to the waterfall.

   Once there, you find yourself in front of a beautiful waterfall. At the top of the waterfall, you see beautiful, colourful blooming flowers. You find the steps that can take you up there to the blooming flowers, and you start climbing up, one step at a time. Some steps have thorns or overgrown grass that don't let you pass, so you have to bend down, pluck these and throw them out of your way.

   You climb a few more steps, and then you see a snake sitting there on your way. You wait until the snake goes away and then go up a few more steps, pulling out few more weeds and thorns along the way.

   Then you come across a big boulder on one of the steps. You try to move it, but can't push it out of your way. You think for a little while, and then you squeeze through the tiny space that is left.

   You reach the top and you discover that the beautiful blooming garden at the top is even more spectacular that you imagined. Your hands are muddy, bruised, and bleeding a little because of all the work you did along the way on the steps, but it all heals as you walk through the miraculous garden.

   That garden is the garden of your dreams and desires. The hurdles on your way are the hurdles you face on your journey to your dreams. Some can be plucked and discarded, some need for you to squeeze past them and get bruised or scratched doing so. There are some that need patience, and just like a snake, they will resolve by themselves.

2. **Take a Breath:** If you feel stressed due to the issues you face, just take some slow deep breaths – this calms the fight or flight response. Take a break and grab a coffee, sitting in your favorite corner of the home/office.
3. **Stay Hydrated:** Drink water and electrolytes. Staying hydrated and having good electrolyte balance has many benefits, including supporting brain function, regulating stress hormones, and regulating the nervous system.
4. **Revisit Your Why:** Remind yourself of your "why," and keep this reason at the forefront of everything. It won't stop the bad days, but it will make them bearable.

RULE 11

# TRUST YOUR INSTINCTS

> *"There is a voice that doesn't use words. Listen."*
> **– Rumi**

Before your head starts to fathom the questions, or the heart the feelings, the gut has already answered them, and the soul already knows it.

We are born with a keen sense of intuition, a way of communicating with our Higher Self way before we learn to communicate with the world. As we learn to communicate with this world, our ability to connect with the inner voice gets pushed back into the subconscious mind. Cultural appropriation makes us focus on the conscious mind at all times, forcing us to heed the obvious the visible facts and to ignore the not-so-obvious truth residing in the subconscious.

The world around us facilitates the disruption of this core connection – the educational system, the workforce, and the authorities in different areas reward the acts of the conscious mind, while deriding and punishing the deeper core wisdom of the subconscious mind. Not only are we conditioned to have razor focus on the conscious mind, we are, surprisingly, conditioned to not only ignore but completely disconnect from the subconscious.

Under the guise of "factual" and "scientific" knowledge, we have long forgotten the significance of intuitive wisdom. We ignore the truth that our mind knows only limited things, and that our instinct, on the other hand, knows everything. Our Higher Self has the wisdom of years, of ages, and of lifetimes. Listening to what we know instinctively will avoid diversions from the right path.

> *"Don't try to comprehend with your mind. Your minds are very limited. Use your intuition."*
>
> **– Madeleine L'Engle**

We can manage fine in our day-to-day lives by pushing our instincts back into the depths of our gut, and yet successfully traverse our paths without friction. Occasionally, it may be enough for those who seek just that. But when we seek more, we have to leave our comfort zone and go into the wilderness of our intuition, where we'll discover the wonder of life, we'll rediscover ourselves.

> *"Intuition doesn't tell you what you want to hear; it tells you what you need to hear."*
>
> **– Sonia Choquette**

## Shakuntala Devi

The "human computer" of our times, Shakuntala Devi was an extraordinarily gifted Indian mathematician known for her uncanny ability to perform complex mathematical calculations mentally, with astonishing speed and accuracy. More inspiring than her knowledge and her resilience is the deep trust she showed in her instincts.

Her innate mathematical skills were evident early in life. Despite having no formal education, she could memorize numbers and perform complex calculations before learning how to write any language. Financial constraints led to the discontinuation of her formal education, and while we may expect it to hinder her growth, it actually was a boon in disguise as she was able to hone in to her own intuition and develop mathematical capabilities by herself.

Her mental calculation and computational talent were unwittingly presented and interpreted as a miracle to be displayed, rather than a prodigious mathematical and scientific skill. As an Indian woman demonstrating such a feat in western male-dominated scientific community, she faced skepticism and prejudice. For someone to have an ability to beat the computational ability of computers in that era with mere mental calculations was an accomplishment beyond imagination.

In the 20th century, Devi was at the frontier of Vedic mathematics, a unique. ancient system originating from India, that consists of techniques for solving complex numerical problems using "sutras," or aphorisms. Despite not being formally integrated into the educational system, Vedic mathematics is gaining popularity in recent times, and in the western world as well.

Although the world knows her as a mental math prodigy – that she was gifted in her ability to devise her own techniques of calculations, the recognition she received and the Guinness World record she held – we could not completely fathom her connection with numbers.

She was often quoted saying she could "feel" the numbers and that the numbers "talk to her." Her faith in this intuitive understanding of math was a subject of research for scientists around the world. She authored books on mathematics for scientists and for students in elementary school, and her computational abilities also gave her an edge in astrological calculations. When asked how she did calculations so quickly, she didn't give a technical answer. Her responses revealed a mix of intuition, pattern recognition, and mental visualization.

Shakuntala Devi's life is a testament to the power of intuition, self-belief, and perseverance. She not only mastered numbers but also refused to let societal norms, gender roles, or personal setbacks define her; she embraced her strengths and her uniqueness. Through her presentations, she not only inspired generations of young women to overcome systemic barriers, but also opened the doors of science, math and technology to women around the world.

This is a reminder that trusting your instincts is not being soft or weak, and that it is actually tapping into a divine warehouse of knowledge and wisdom.

*"Your intuition knows what to do. The trick is getting your head to shut up so you can hear."*

**– Louise Smith**

## "Spidey" Senses

Our brain has two distinct, partially interconnected nervous systems: the central nervous system and the enteric nervous system. The enteric nervous system is the signal that our gut sends to our brain, by the way of "feeling" or "Spidey senses." Sometimes you may have felt "butterflies in your stomach" due to anxiety or excitement, or you may have experienced your "heart is sinking into the stomach" or that "there was a hole or a pit in the stomach" due to fear or shock. At other times, without much of these feelings or a reason behind these feelings, you may have sensed "something's just not right." Sometimes it may be that you're not "getting good vibes." All of these are signs of having a gut feeling, or having an instinct about something. Through our senses, our body gathers information and our gut carries as much of the information as the brain does.

**How most leaders make decisions**

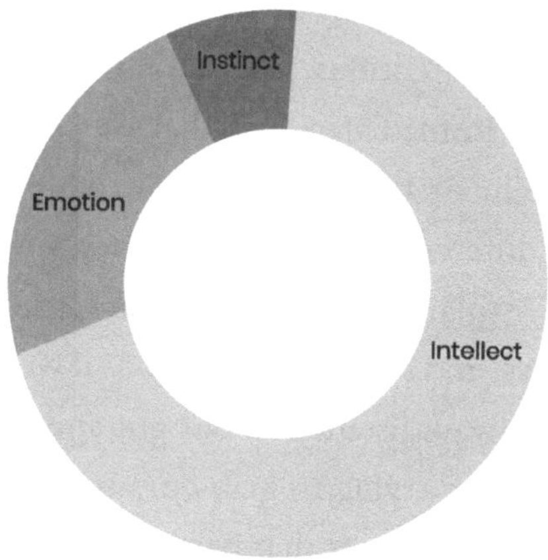


As we have seen in Chapter 3, the process of decision making involves many parts of the cortex and the hippocampus in the brain. Our reliance on the logical process of decision making is not wrong at all – that is one of the primary functions of the brain. At times, we tend to listen to our heart and forgo the logic in the brain, especially in emotionally involved situations and issues within close relationships. While all of this takes time to process, the enteric nervous system is the first to respond by sending out a signal, telling us ever so quietly, what to do in a particular situation.

How many times has it happened that you meet a person, and even if you're meeting them for the first time, and even if you don't know much about them, you don't get a good feeling in your gut? The person may be saying all the right things that you were looking to hear, and yet your antennae go up and you sense something is not right. Sometimes it may be a certain friendliness of a colleague or a manager or senior executive, and at other times, you may not be able to trust someone about truly representing you correctly in a meeting. Sometimes you may not feel right about a decision you made, and you feel sick to your stomach thinking about it. That is your instinct telling you to beware.

As women, we are also acutely aware of the energy that people carry, and through that their intentions. We can also sense the energy that a place carries, and the immediate sense that our gut sends out to us is different from the fight or flight response of the hippocampus and the amygdala. The core difference is that the instinct is immediate and often fleeting, and with no explanation, while the fear response in fight or flight is something that stays, and starts giving reasons if we try to get rid of it or ignore it. If we have always listened to our gut and to our instincts, they may linger around longer, trying to grab our attention, even showing up every time we are thinking about that particular issue.

If we have always ignored our instincts then to be able to differentiate between instinct and fear is a crucial step. Not so surprisingly, it is easier to silence the whisper of the gut as compared to the loud screaming of fear. Time and experience bring us this awareness, and helps us differentiate between the two. For those who have always believed in and nurtured their instincts, there is no question about finding this difference, because they just *know* it.

We are all born with a very robust instinct, but we need to nurture it and care for it. All it takes is paying heed when it speaks to us. Ignoring it is the best way to diminish the instincts. Reminding ourselves to stay in touch with our inner core is nurturing for the soul and for the instinct. Tuning in to our intuition and listening to our instinct more frequently than men do is what differentiates us and gives us an edge.

> *"Rock bottom became the solid foundation on which I rebuilt my life."*
> **– J.K. Rowling**

## J.K. Rowling

If intuition was suppressed by J.K. Rowling, the author of the *Harry Potter* book series, not only would the world be deprived of one of the most influential authors, but new age literature would also be incomplete without her work seeing the light of the day.

Growing up in a small village on the English-Welsh border, Joanne Rowling wrote her first story at six and her first novel at 11. She continued writing throughout school and university. Inspiration struck while on a train to London, when she was struck by an idea of a boy wizard who went to wizarding school. Harry Potter and Hogwarts came out of nowhere, tugging hard onto her imagination and in her gut, she simply knew that she had to write the story as seven books. For a writer, it was an unusual day to have no pen or paper handy.

As she started a five-year journey of writing the first of the series, there were no lack of challenges. At 25, losing her mother to multiple sclerosis completely shattered her, and she still regrets not having been given the opportunity to tell her mother about her Harry Potter book series. During this time of personal loss, depression, and emotional instability, she moved to Portugal, got married, and had her first daughter.

The marriage did not work out, and she moved with her daughter and the first few chapters of the book to Scotland. Financial hardships forced her to work as a teacher, and write in her spare time, with her baby in tow. With the menial salary she received and the state benefits for a single mom she could barely make ends meet. Clinical depression and suicidal thoughts tormented her as she struggled to write and bring her dream to reality. At one point she could not even afford to buy a computer or a typewriter, nor could she afford to get a photocopy of her manuscript and novel to be sent out to publishers. Instead, she manually typed out 12 copies and sent it to her literary agent to be sent to publishers.

Most of her writing in the Harry Potter book was still on the lines of her intuitive feelings that she envisioned on that train journey a few years ago. The publishers rejected these, asking her to focus on finding a job instead. They emphasized the lack of demand for such children's books, implying the notion that she was not a good author. She did not let the rejections faze her, as she apparently was already at the lowest point in her life, and knew the only way ahead was up.

Finally, her patience and perseverance paid off when the Bloomsbury publishing house in the U.K. agreed to publish her. Publishers feared that such a book by a woman would not appeal to young boys, however, who seemed to be a major target audience for the book, so she gave in to the request to change the name on the book from "Joanne Rowling" to "J.K. Rowling."

In June 1997, Bloomsbury published *Harry Potter and the Philosopher's Stone* in the UK and it did fairly well. In August 1998, the book was published in the US as *Harry Potter and the Sorcerer's Stone*, and that completely changed the trajectory of the book, as well as Rowling's life.

Harry Potter became a phenomenon, and the next six books of the series took her another 10 years to write and publish. During this time, the movies based on the books were released as well. The 17 years of her life that she had given to this single dream of writing the Harry Potter series had finally paid off, and J.K. Rowling became as much of a global phenomenon as the characters in her book. Seventeen years of faith, dedication, and single-minded focus. Seventeen years of complete faith in her inner voice and her instincts. From the pits of poverty, she rose to fame to become the first author who became a billionaire through writing alone.

Rowling founded Lumos, an international children's charity that fights for a child's right to a family by transforming care systems around the world, and she continues to write for diverse age groups. Her subsequent books have all been adapted into television series, and she continues to write the adult series under the pseudonym of Robert Galbraith. She has also written plays and screenplays.

In memory of her mother, she supports research and care for multiple sclerosis patients in Edinburgh. She is emblematic of trusting her gut and listening to her intuitions, in spite of being repeatedly dismissed and underestimated – and that's where lies the foundation of her literary empire.

## Henrietta Leavitt

Knowing how life works or how intuitions arise may not be sufficient enough to truly tap into the power of tuning in. It is a road paved with enormous resistance, and yet we know of several trailblazers who proceeded with complete faith in their instincts, smashing the myth along the way that intuition does not belong in science.

Intuition is frequently relied upon by many scientists to pioneer new paths in science, to get answers to questions that seem impossible to understand, thereby proving that intuition is not only compatible with science but also is essential to it.

Henrietta Leavitt was an American astronomer whose work fundamentally changed our understanding of the size and scale of the universe. Her discoveries and her ability to listen to her intuition, despite pushback, laid the foundations for the astronomical breakthroughs of the 20th century.

Leavitt studied at Oberlin College and Radcliffe College (then the women's counterpart to Harvard), where she developed an interest in astronomy, in spite of the many institutional and social constraints placed on women at the time. Women were admitted to universities, but were given the designation of "Harvard Computers," essentially doing scientific calculations and analysis, with very low pay and without due credit being accorded to them. The academic titles and the rights over the results of such analysis, were reserved for men n the field.

In 1893, Leavitt began working at the Harvard College Observatory as one such "Harvard Computer" under Edward Charles Pickering, analysing and cataloging astronomical data from photographic plates. While men were in charge of operation of telescopes and the field observations, Leavitt performed the tedious task of examining the photographic plates for the brightness of stars.

> *"Good instincts usually tell you what to do long before your head has figured it out."*
>
> **– Michael Burke**

On one such duty, analyzing variable stars in the Small Magellanic Cloud, Leavitt made a groundbreaking discovery. She found a direct correlation between the period of a Cepheid star's brightness fluctuations and its intrinsic luminosity (true brightness). The Cepheid variable star is a type of star that pulsates regularly, changing in brightness over a period of time. Leavitt's intuition told her that there was a hidden rhythm in the Cepheid stars, and thus the period-luminosity relationship was born. This became the foundation for the period-luminosity law of astronomy (later known as Leavitt's Law). She discovered that by observing how long a Cepheid takes to brighten and dim, astronomers could determine how bright it truly is. Comparing this with how bright it appears from Earth allowed them to calculate its distance.

Prior to this discovery, the astronomers had no reliable way to measure distances between far away celestial objects and galaxies beyond the Milky Way. This discovery was crucial in enabling scientists to accurately measure distances in space, and it laid the foundations of an expanding universe as a possibility in the astronomical community. Her work enabled the astronomers to establish the cosmic vastness, and inspired physicists and astronomers alike.

At a time when scientists all over the globe struggled to find ways to understand spatial distances and cosmic vastness, Leavitt used her intuition to identify a cosmic scale from pattern recognition through the plot of brightness and time. While the likes of Albert Einstein have posthumously acknowledged the importance of her discovery, she was simultaneously robbed of her right to the Nobel Prize. Posthumously she was recognized for her contributions to science and astronomy, and she demonstrated the importance of the amalgamation of intuition and science.

*"Intuition is a very powerful thing, more powerful than intellect, in my opinion."*

**– Steve Jobs**

From ancient times, there have been many other remarkable women throughout history – across science, math, arts and literature – who demonstrated intuitive capabilities and an inner conviction to follow them.

From Hypathia of Alexandria, the philosopher, astronomer, and mathematician, to Emmy Noether, a pioneer in math and physics, there are many examples of prominent women tuning in to their intuitive abilities. The Noether theorem, which relates to symmetry and conservation laws, was a breakthrough that Emmy attributed to a deep instinctive feel of algebra.

Barbara McClintock, a pioneer in genetics, intuitively knew that genes could move, not stay fixed as most scientists believed, and discovered transposons (jumping genes).

Lisa Meitner, a nuclear physicist, had intuitive insight into atomic behavior, and when the available knowledge and evidence didn't fit classical physics, she sensed the possibility of the atom splitting, leading to the concept of nuclear fission, and laying the foundations for nuclear energy as well as nuclear weapons.

It was a very important discovery for someone living through the world wars and having to flee Nazi Germany, and despite the unfairness of the scientific community, which awarded the Nobel Prize only to her male co-scientists, she maintained a strong advocacy for the ethical use of science and scientific discoveries.

Paleontologist Mary Anning attributes many of her discoveries of dinosaur fossils to intuition, as it was as if she instinctively knew where to look for them.

### Intuition is not the sole domain of women.

Many well-recognized men and women from diverse fields, not just science and math, have similarly relied heavily on intuitive knowledge. Leonardo da Vinci, Albert Einstein, and Salvador are just a few of them. But it is important to remember that it is not just these great discoveries that intuition can be relied upon for; intuition or instinct is something that comes to our aid for every decision of our life, big or small.

> *"Instinct is a marvelous thing. It can neither be explained nor ignored."*
>
> **– Agatha Christie**

Intuition is not the sole domain of women; it is something that men and women both have. Unquestionably, instinct is one of the most basic characteristics of any living being, from plants and insects to birds and animals, to human beings and even nature itself. It is truly the sixth sense – and the most important one at that – for survival, safety, and growth. Women have managed to stay in touch with this slightly more than men have, and it seems to be more of an evolutionary physical change in the body of men as compared to women.

Have you ever noticed an indoor plant beginning to grow towards the nearest window in the house? This occurs because the plant instinctively knows to reach out for the sun.

Minutes or hours before a natural calamity, animals and birds start to flee the area, or they seem uneasy and impatient. Whether it is an earthquake or a tsunami, fish, birds, and other animals show a very peculiar behaviour, and even the most sophisticated scientific equipment fails to predict the calamities with as much of an accuracy as the instincts of these creatures. All these living beings are still in touch with their inner core. It is only the worldly-wise humans, the top-most-ranking creatures in the evolutionary phase, that have forgotten to listen to their instincts.

> *"The intuitive mind is a sacred gift and the rational mind is a faithful servant. We have created a society that honors the servant and has forgotten the gift."*
>
> **– Albert Einstein**

Intuition can tap on your shoulder during a major issue or a small one, and the voice may be louder or smaller in either of these scenarios. It is a tap that may feel like a brush, it may be a voice that is a whisper. Training yourself to listen to this voice is one of the best gifts we can give to ourselves – not only does it keep us safe, but it also helps us make the right decision and plays a crucial role in navigating our life.

Our instinct can help us sense our surroundings and people, helps us with analysing and assessing the complete picture of any situation, and nudges us towards the right decision. It also helps us build meaningful connections with people. Overall, it would be right to say that intuition helps us to see the map of our lives, past, present and future.

It is a compass that we have deep inside us, one that could guide our every move, if only we would listen. The world puts a veil on this compass, and our clouded vision prevents us from knowing the compass is there, or even accessing the compass at the right time. Recognizing the significance of intuition, and then working towards it, can help in rebuilding that connection. Intuition is empowering, liberating, and connecting at the same time, freeing us from our fears and self-imposed restrictions, and connecting to our inner core, our Higher Self, and to our partners, children, friends, and family.

If you can do only one thing for yourself, let it be learning to trust your instincts and to listen to your intuition. Having your intuition guide you is the one big difference between winning and success, and it is one crucial point from where the road to fulfillment begins.

## Taking Action:

1. **Meditate:** Do Brahma Muhurta meditation or meditation within 45 minutes before or after sunrise. Rise up early in the morning – the body will revolt at first and hold you onto the warm coziness of the bed, but as you get into the routine, the process will become easier.

   Find a nice spot in your home and light a candle. Sit in padmasana, and do inverted U-shaped breathing. Hold your right hand close to your face – you will be using this hand to close one nostril at a time. Start by exhaling through the left nostril, then inhale through the same nostril, close that nostril and exhale through the right nostril. Inhale through the same nostril, then switch the nostril and exhale again through the left. Repeat this for a few minutes.

2. **Chant:** Do Om chanting 21 times. Sit with your eyes closed, and let the guidance come. Imagine it arriving towards you from the deep darkness of the Universe. It may feel like nothing but positive energy at first, but after a few days of practice, your answers will start arriving along with that energy.

3. **Do Some Writing:** After the meditation write down all thoughts that came to your mind.

4. **Move Forward:** If you identify some guidance that you were looking for, put it into action. Express gratitude for receiving the divine guidance.

RULE 12

# ROCK THOSE HEELS

> *"Women have always been the strong ones of the world."*
> **– Coco Chanel**

Your crown does not come from inheritance – it comes from going through the fire of hardships and the gardens of fulfillment.

It's only when a rock is exposed to extreme temperatures, compressed for years, and passed through the grinding machines, that a diamond is born, bright and precious enough to adorn the crown. It is emblematic that the substantiveness of a diamond comes from what it went through to be where it is.

Life, like light, is dual in nature and is made up of waves, as well as particles. We all have to go through the crests of joy and the troughs of struggle, and some people ride those waves and some get tossed around. The choice of how we find the light of our life is ours. The particles are the traits of our character, so the stronger the traits, the brighter the light. And in our dark challenging times, they bring the light of hope and promise.

The rules in this book are the steps that we can take to enable the light within us to shine bright. To alight the path to our goals and to bring us all that we desire. When we step into our light, we rock those heels and take strides into our manifestations.

Manifesting our desires is a simple but tedious process – simple because it is fundamentally straightforward, and tedious because this simplicity is something that is easily forgotten by our convoluted minds. We all desire success, growth, joy, happiness, and most importantly, love. There is no question that we all desire to find meaning in our lives and to live up to the purpose of our lives. This is the Japanese concept of *ikigai*, living in the centre of purpose, joy, contentment, and fulfilment. Use this book to find your *ikigai*.

## Manifestation Through a Mindset of Abundance

Being successful as a man means being working towards excellence at work and in the network, having a loving family, and becoming the most powerful person.

Being successful as a woman means working towards excellence at work and in life, being an ideal leader, and at the same time, the best mom, best daughter, best friend to your girls, and making sure you are contributing to making the world a better place – because after all, what are we leaving behind for our children?

And we must do so wearing a ravishing dress and high heels!

Simple goals of the parallel lives of men demand different elemental rules, as author Robert Greene highlights in his book, *The 48 Laws of Power*. The complexity of women's brains desires a complete, interconnected circle of life, and therefore, complex goals, which require different rules that we have been discussing in this book.

These rules are a sacred path to our goals, malleable to suit each one of us in our own way, and crucial for women in succeeding on this sacred journey to and through our dreams and our desires.

The most important ground rule, though, is that the dreams and desires are our own. You cannot take someone else's journey; you cannot traverse someone else's path. We live in a world of social media, where we see other people's dreams, desires, and achievements all the time. At times, parents, teachers, siblings, spouses, and friends will give us different ideas of what our lives should look like. Experts and influencers, and movies and media will sometimes show us glimpses of an ideal life. But it is their life to revel in – you can't live someone else's dream if you don't belong to it.

We were born knowing our purpose and our dreams, and as we grew older, the noise around us muffled our inner voice. Somewhere along the way, the intelligence got replaced by intellect and we started focusing on honing in on our intellect. The dissecting nature of the intellect wants to analyze everything, quantify everything, compare everything, and evaluate everything based on observations, not based on instinct. By trusting your intuition, and identifying your purpose, you forsake the conditioning of the world and ground yourself in your truth. Because once you find that, the friction reduces. What you seek is seeking you – the path that is yours is calling you and waiting for you to discover it.

Another law of the universe is the Law of Abundance. There is enough of everything that anyone could ever want in the Universe, and there is enough for everyone to have what they truly desire. This truth gets suppressed by the world that functions on the principle of scarcity. Every business and every entrepreneur is taught to believe in the law of scarcity, and use it as a bait in attracting consumers. No matter which side of the table we are on, this is how we drift away from the mindset of abundance. Creation is abundant, and so are the possibilities. The abundance mindset eliminates insecurity and fear and imparts to us the ability to take bold actions and bold decisions.

> *"And, when you want something, all the universe conspires in helping you to achieve it."*
> **– Paulo Coelho**

The most famous line in *The Alchemist* by Paulo Coelho, somehow became one of the most important statements of our lives. The concept of manifestation existed prior to Coelho writing about it, but Coelho's words imbibe the essence of both the Law of Attraction and the Law of Abundance.

One fact that is elucidated in ancient texts throughout history, and lost in translation into modern languages, is this:

> *"A prayer of gratitude for receiving something is way more powerful than a prayer asking for something."*

## Manifestation Through Being

When you act with discipline, even when no one is watching, you are worth trusting. Being the best version of yourself at all times, though, is not an easy feat – when you begin the journey of embracing your true self, there will be fatigue, impatience, frustration and fear gnawing at the back of your mind.

> *"Her own thoughts and reflections were habitually her best companions."*
> **– Jane Austen**

Only when you face your reality do you become available for transformation. It takes immense courage to see yourself truly the way you are and crossing this first hurdle brings you to the two major hurdles: accepting yourself and embracing yourself.

The Japanese concept of *wabi-sabi* expounds the beauty of the fleeting, changeable, and imperfect nature of things. It specifically highlights that beauty lies not in perfection, but in the flawed incompleteness of being. The theory of Aligned Perfection discussed in Chapter 8 alludes to this concept of *wabi-sabi*. Only when we embrace our incomplete, flawed selves can we actually move closer to growth and development for ourselves.

Perfect people don't exist on this earth – as per the Hindu culture and concept of *moksha*, your existence on this earth is because you have to learn some lessons and evolve into better beings. If you're perfect, and don't have anything to evolve into, you should attain *moksha* or liberation.

### Love yourself first and everything will fall into place.

Many affirmations and journaling or meditation techniques focus on manifestation through being. When we embrace being ourselves out in the public, not just at home or in private, we are going to be judged by others, but it is testament to our character. Being true to ourselves, without prejudice, gives us a unique confidence and charisma that cannot be ignored.

You may be detested for this, not because of who you are, but because you make others realize who they can be, but choose not to be. Those who have chosen the path of deception to move ahead at work can never know the taste of a fulfilling life. You are a glaring example to them of the roads not taken, the mountains not climbed, and the life not lived, and that is what pushes some people away from you. They would rather live in the comfort of the lies they tell themselves everyday than to face their truths.

### Be the energy you want to attract.

While you push people away people with your brutal honesty and by being yourself, you also attract the right kind of like-minded people whose core values align with that of yours. These are the allies that you should tread with, on the same path but on different journeys, and help and support each other along the way. What is crucial to finding your tribe is choosing the right alliances, because without the right people, you have left yourself vulnerable to vultures.

Men and women are different, but they are not enemies. Sometimes men may be against the growth of a woman, and sometimes women may be the ones against their own. When you build your dream, and get wounded along the way, the knife could be wielded very well by another woman who can't see you succeed, and the healing bandage may very well be in the hand of a man. It is prudent that, on your journey filled with hurdles, you remain aware and wise.

Trouble will not always come wearing a tie and a suit. Don't be skeptical of everyone around you, but use your judgement, your experience, and your intuition to guide you. Understanding this is crucial.

### Manifestation through becoming.

Embodying the person whom we will become is a crucial step in attracting our dreams. It is living and breathing our manifestations in real time that will attract them to us from the deepest crevices of the Universe.

As we embark on the journey to success, and truly learn to embrace ourselves, we need to be bold enough to embody our future self. As we leave all the challenges, struggles, and the victimhood behind, we will make room for more of ourselves. Battered, incomplete, and flawed, and yet embodying our future, successful, fulfilled version of ourselves, we invite that future to come to the present, invite growth, and invite change. All the negativities fall apart, all the attacks on us fall apart, and we rise, not because we were allowed to by those who tried to jeopardize our path earlier, but *despite* them.

We rise because we are ready and emboldened to claim our rightful place, and it is a place that no one can take away from us. It is not about surviving the hardships; it is about the reassertion of our strength that could not be extinguished by the vengeful minds. Rising, in this manner, is an act of self-respect, and it empowers us to reclaim our narrative, our power, and our destiny from those who think they can shape our lives according to their whims. It means stepping out of shadows of pain and rejection and into the light of our own potential.

Embodying our future self is an arduous process of provoking ourselves to shed the fears and the negative emotions of today. Embodying our future self compels us to rise above everything – internal as well as external – that is holding us back. It is the process of becoming who we aspire to be, and achieving what we aspire to achieve. As we fully realize our boldest, biggest, unhinged dreams, we make the energy of the Universe flow through us.

> *"Life is a gift, and it offers us the privilege, opportunity, and responsibility to give something back by becoming more."*
>
> **– Tony Robbins**

It's been far too long that we have been in our cocoons, and it's been way too long that we have been standing in the boxes that were designed for us. It is high time we dust ourselves off, break those invisible shackles that we have accepted without question, and stand up. How the world would be different if more women owned up to our strengths, stepped out of those boxes, and rocked those heels!

Stop playing small to remain acceptable, and let the loud clanking of your heels announce that you have arrived.

*"Do not feel lonely – the entire universe is inside you. Stop acting so small. You are the universe in ecstatic motion. Set your life on fire."*

**– Rumi**